# Bradshaw's Diary and Travellers' Companion.
## Being a revised and improved edition of Bradshaw's Diary and Route Record, etc.

George Bradshaw

## The BiblioLife Network

This project was made possible in part by the BiblioLife Network (BLN), a project aimed at addressing some of the huge challenges facing book preservationists around the world. The BLN includes libraries, library networks, archives, subject matter experts, online communities and library service providers. We believe every book ever published should be available as a high-quality print reproduction; printed on- demand anywhere in the world. This insures the ongoing accessibility of the content and helps generate sustainable revenue for the libraries and organizations that work to preserve these important materials.

The following book is in the "public domain" and represents an authentic reproduction of the text as printed by the original publisher. While we have attempted to accurately maintain the integrity of the original work, there are sometimes problems with the original book or micro-film from which the books were digitized. This can result in minor errors in reproduction. Possible imperfections include missing and blurred pages, poor pictures, markings and other reproduction issues beyond our control. Because this work is culturally important, we have made it available as part of our commitment to protecting, preserving, and promoting the world's literature.

## GUIDE TO FOLD-OUTS, MAPS and OVERSIZED IMAGES

In an online database, page images do not need to conform to the size restrictions found in a printed book. When converting these images back into a printed bound book, the page sizes are standardized in ways that maintain the detail of the original. For large images, such as fold-out maps, the original page image is split into two or more pages.

Guidelines used to determine the split of oversize pages:

• Some images are split vertically; large images require vertical and horizontal splits.
• For horizontal splits, the content is split left to right.
• For vertical splits, the content is split from top to bottom.
• For both vertical and horizontal splits, the image is processed from top left to bottom right.

10849. c 15

# BRADSHAW'S

## Diary and Travellers' Companion.

BEING

A REVISED AND IMPROVED EDITION OF BRADSHAW'S
DIARY AND ROUTE RECORD.

COMPRISING

TABLES FOR RECORDING PARTICULARS OF JOURNEYS, ROUTES,
FARES, TRAVELLING EXPENSES, LUGGAGE, HOTELS, PLACES
VISITED, ENGAGEMENTS, JOTTINGS OR LOG OF LAND AND
SEA TOURS, ETC.   RAILWAY STATION AND STREET PLANS
OF LONDON AND PARIS, TOGETHER WITH A SELECTION
OF MISCELLANEOUS INFORMATION FOR TRAVELLERS AND
TOURISTS, &C.

PUBLISHED AND SOLD BY

W. J. ADAMS, RAILWAY PUBLISHER, 59, FLEET STREET, E.C.,

BRADSHAW & BLACKLOCK, ALBERT SQUARE, MANCHESTER.

And to be had at all Railway Stations.

# BRADSHAW'S
# Diary and Travellers' Companion.

THE leading object of this "Diary" is to furnish Travellers and Tourists with a simple and ready means of recording such matters of information and reference as the following ;—

*Particulars of journeys, routes, luggage, hotels.*
*Travelling expenses.*
*Places visited, either on business or pleasure.*
*Engagements or appointments made during the journey.*
*Jottings or Log of Land and Sea Tours, &c.*

The particulars, therefore, which Travellers during their journey or tour may derive and enter under the various headings in the tables comprised in this Diary, may doubtless be found interesting as well as useful for subsequent reference, inasmuch as it will be seen that provision is made for a systematic registering of travelling detail of almost every character. This "Diary and Companion" may, therefore, probably supply a *desideratum* which will be found acceptable, and of general service to the travelling community ; and form a suitable companion or pendant to "Bradshaw" and other Guide Books.

For Ladies, travelling alone, and without a previous experience of the journey, a reference by them to the columns relating to time, fares and journeys, which in such cases can previously be filled up, will be found very useful.

With the view of rendering this work attractive, and at the same time generally instructive, a selection of valuable information and statistics has been arranged especially for this work, in such a form as to be easily perused by Travellers, &c.

A Railway Station and Street Plan of London and Paris designed upon a new principle (specially for this Diary and Travellers' Companion), will be found at each end of the book.

# CONTENTS.

| DATE. | NAMES, &c., OF PARTIES TRAVELLING TOGETHER. |
| --- | --- |
| | |
| | |
| | |
| | |
| | |
| | |
| | |
| | |
| | |
| | |
| | |
| | |
| | |
| | |
| | |
| | |
| | |

4

| Date. | Names, &c., of Parties Travelling Together. |
|-------|---------------------------------------------|
|       | ............................................. |
|       | ............................................. |
|       | ............................................. |
|       | ............................................. |
|       | ............................................. |
|       | ............................................. |
|       | ............................................. |
|       | ............................................. |
|       | ............................................. |
|       | ............................................. |
|       | ............................................. |
|       | ............................................. |
|       | ............................................. |
|       | ............................................. |

## DIARY OF

| Date of Journey. | From | To | TIME OF JOURNEY. | |
|---|---|---|---|---|
| | | | Departure | Arrival |
| | | | | |

# JOURNEYS.

| Class. | (A) PASSENGER FARES. Amount. | | | Total No. Packages. | (B) LUGGAGE. Paid for Overweight. | | | (C) SUNDRIES. Cab or Bus Fare, Porterage, Refreshments, Bookstalls, &c. | | | Distance of Journey. | CONVEYANCE, ROUTE, &c. Name of Railway Company, Steamer, or Coach. |
|---|---|---|---|---|---|---|---|---|---|---|---|---|
| | £ | s. | d. | | £ | s. | d. | £ | s. | d. | Miles. | |
| | | | | | | | | | | | | |

| Date of Journey. | From | To | TIME OF JOURNEY. | |
|---|---|---|---|---|
| | | | Departure. | Arrival. |

# JOURNEYS.

| (A) PASSENGER FARES. | | (B) LUGGAGE. | | (C) SUNDRIES. | Distance of Journey. | CONVEYANCE, ROUTE, &c. |
|---|---|---|---|---|---|---|
| Class. | Amount. | Total No. Packages. | Paid for Overweight. | Cab or Bus Fare, Porterage, Refreshments, Bookstalls, &c. | | Name of Railway Company, Steamer, or Coach. |
| | £    s.    d. | | £    s.    d. | £    s.    d. | Miles. | |

| Date of Journey. | From | To | TIME OF JOURNEY. | |
|---|---|---|---|---|
| | | | Departure. | Arrival. |

## JOURNEYS.

| Class. | (A) PASSENGER FARES. Amount. | | | Total No. Packages. | (B) LUGGAGE. Paid for Overweight. | | | (C) SUNDRIES. Cab or Bus Fare, Porterage, Refreshments, Bookstalls, &c. | | | Distance of Journey. | CONVEYANCE, ROUTE, &c. Name of Railway Company, Steamer, or Coach. |
|---|---|---|---|---|---|---|---|---|---|---|---|---|
| | £ | s. | d. | | £ | s. | d. | £ | s. | d. | Miles. | |

| Date of Journey. | From | To | TIME OF JOURNEY. | |
|---|---|---|---|---|
| | | | Departure. | Arrival. |

# JOURNEYS.

| (A) PASSENGER FARES. | | (B) LUGGAGE. | | (C) SUNDRIES. Cab or Bus Fare, Porterage, Refreshments, Bookstalls, &c. | Distance of Journey. | CONVEYANCE, ROUTE, &c. Name of Railway Company, Steamer, or Coach. |
|---|---|---|---|---|---|---|
| Class. | Amount. | Total No. Packages. | Paid for Overweight. | | | |
| | £   s.   d. | | £   s.   d. | £   s.   d. | Miles. | |

# DIARY OF

| Date of Journey. | From | To | TIME OF JOURNEY. | |
|---|---|---|---|---|
| | | | Departure. | Arrival. |

# JOURNEYS.

| (A) PASSENGER FARES. | | (B) LUGGAGE. | | (C) SUNDRIES. | Distance of Journey. | CONVEYANCE, ROUTE, &c. |
|---|---|---|---|---|---|---|
| Class. | Amount. | Total No. Packages. | Paid for Overweight. | Cab or Bus Fare, Porterage, Refreshments, Bookstalls, &c. | | Name of Railway Company, Steamer, or Coach. |
| | £   s.   d. | . | £   s.   d. | £   s.   d. | Miles. | |

## HOTELS AND PRIVATE LODGINGS.

| Town or Place. | Name of Hotel or Address of Private Lodging. | TIME AT HOTEL OR LODGINGS. | |
| --- | --- | --- | --- |
| | | Date of arrival. | Date of leaving. |
| | | | |

# HOTELS AND PRIVATE LODGINGS.

| (D) Total Amount paid for Hotels or Lodgings. | | | Number or Name of Rooms occupied. | REMARKS as to Hotel or Lodgings. |
|---|---|---|---|---|
| £ | s. | d. | | |
| | | | | |

# HOTELS AND PRIVATE LODGINGS

| Town or Place. | Name of Hotel or Address of Private Lodging. | TIME AT HOTEL OR LODGINGS. | |
| --- | --- | --- | --- |
| | | Date of arrival. | Date of leaving. |
| | | | |

# HOTELS AND PRIVATE LODGINGS.

| (D) Total Amount paid for Hotels or Lodgings. | | | Number or Name of Rooms occupied. | REMARKS as to Hotel or Lodgings. |
|---|---|---|---|---|
| £ | s. | d. | | |

# HOTELS AND PRIVATE LODGINGS

| Town or Place. | Name of Hotel or Address of Private Lodging. | TIME AT HOTEL OR LODGINGS. | |
|---|---|---|---|
| | | Date of arrival. | Date of leaving. |
| | | | |

# HOTELS AND PRIVATE LODGINGS.

| (D) Total Amount paid for Hotels or Lodgings. | | | Number or Name of Rooms occupied. | REMARKS as to Hotel or Lodgings. |
|---|---|---|---|---|
| £ | s. | d. | | |

# HOTELS AND PRIVATE LODGINGS.

| Town or Place. | Name of Hotel or Address of Private Lodging. | TIME AT HOTEL OR LODGINGS. | |
|---|---|---|---|
| | | Date of arrival. | Date of leaving. |
| | | | |

# HOTELS AND PRIVATE LODGINGS.

| (D) Total Amount paid for Hotels or Lodgings. | | | Number or Name of Rooms occupied. | REMARKS as to Hotel or Lodgings. |
|---|---|---|---|---|
| £ | s. | d. | | |
| | | | | |

# HOTELS AND PRIVATE LODGINGS.

| Town or Place. | Name of Hotel or Address of Private Lodging. | TIME AT HOTEL OR LODGINGS. | |
| --- | --- | --- | --- |
| | | Date of arrival. | Date of leaving. |
| | | | |

# HOTELS AND PRIVATE LODGINGS.

| (D) Total Amount paid for Hotels or Lodgings. | | | Number or Name of Rooms occupied. | REMARKS as to Hotel or Lodgings. |
|---|---|---|---|---|
| £ | s. | d. | | |
| | | | | |

# TABLE OF EXPENDITURE.

| Date. | Expenses of Journey per A B C Columns. | | | Expenses of Hotel or Private Lodgings, per Column D. | | | Sundry Expenses at Town or Place. | | | TOTAL Expenditure. | | |
|---|---|---|---|---|---|---|---|---|---|---|---|---|
| | £ | s. | d. | £ | s. | d. | £ | s. | d. | £ | s. | d. |
| | | | | | | | | | | | | |

# TABLE OF EXPENDITURE.

| Date. | Expenses of Journey per A B C Columns. | | | Expenses of Hotel or Private Lodgings, per Column D. | | | Sundry Expenses at Town or Place. | | | TOTAL Expenditure. | | |
|---|---|---|---|---|---|---|---|---|---|---|---|---|
| | £ | s. | d. | £ | s. | d. | £ | s. | d. | £ | s. | d. |
| | | | | | | | | | | | | |
| | | | | | | | | | | | | |
| | | | | | | | | | | | | |
| | | | | | | | | | | | | |
| | | | | | | | | | | | | |
| | | | | | | | | | | | | |
| | | | | | | | | | | | | |
| | | | | | | | | | | | | |
| | | | | | | | | | | | | |
| | | | | | | | | | | | | |
| | | | | | | | | | | | | |
| | | | | | | | | | | | | |
| | | | | | | | | | | | | |
| | | | | | | | | | | | | |
| | | | | | | | | | | | | |

# TABLE OF EXPENDITURE.

| Date. | | Expenses of Journey per A B C Columns. | | | Expenses of Hotel or Private Lodgings, per Column D. | | | Sundry Expenses at Town or Place. | | | TOTAL Expenditure. | | |
|---|---|---|---|---|---|---|---|---|---|---|---|---|---|
| | | £ | s. | d. | £ | s. | d. | £ | s. | d. | £ | s. | d. |
| | | | | | | | | | | | | | |

# TABLE OF EXPENDITURE.

| Date. | | Expenses of Journey per A B C Columns. | | | Expenses of Hotel or Private Lodgings, per Column D. | | | Sundry Expenses at Town or Place. | | | TOTAL Expenditure. | | |
|---|---|---|---|---|---|---|---|---|---|---|---|---|---|
| | | £ | s. | d. | £ | s. | d. | £ | s. | d. | £ | s. | d. |
| | | | | | | | | | | | | | |

# GENERAL DIARY.

| DATE. | PLACES AND PERSONS VISITED, EACH DAY, ENGAGEMENTS, &c. |
| --- | --- |
|  |  |

# GENERAL DIARY.

| DATE. | PLACES AND PERSONS VISITED, EACH DAY, ENGAGEMENTS, &c. |
|-------|--------------------------------------------------------|
|       |                                                        |

# GENERAL DIARY.

| DATE. | PLACES AND PERSONS VISITED, EACH DAY, ENGAGEMENTS, &c. |
|-------|------------------------------------------------------|
|       |                                                      |

# GENERAL DIARY.

| DATE. | PLACES AND PERSONS VISITED, EACH DAY, ENGAGEMENTS, &c. |
|---|---|
|  |  |

# GENERAL DIARY.

| DATE. | PLACES AND PERSONS VISITED, EACH DAY, ENGAGEMENTS, &c. |
|---|---|
|  |  |

# GENERAL DIARY.

| Date. | PLACES AND PERSONS VISITED, EACH DAY, ENGAGEMENTS, &c. |
|---|---|
|  |  |

# GENERAL DIARY.

| DATE. | PLACES AND PERSONS VISITED, EACH DAY, ENGAGEMENTS, &c. |
| --- | --- |
|  |  |

# GENERAL DIARY.

| Date. | PLACES AND PERSONS VISITED, EACH DAY, ENGAGEMENTS, &c. |
| --- | --- |
|  |  |

# GENERAL DIARY.

| DATE. | PLACES AND PERSONS VISITED, EACH DAY, ENGAGEMENTS, &c. |
|-------|--------------------------------------------------------|
|       |                                                        |

# GENERAL DIARY.

| DATE. | PLACES AND PERSONS VISITED, EACH DAY, ENGAGEMENTS, &c. |
|---|---|
|  |  |

# GENERAL DIARY.

| DATE. | PLACES AND PERSONS VISITED, EACH DAY, ENGAGEMENTS, &c. |
|-------|--------------------------------------------------------|
|       |                                                        |

# GENERAL DIARY.

| Date. | PLACES AND PERSONS VISITED, EACH DAY, ENGAGEMENTS, &c. |
| --- | --- |
| | |

# JOTTINGS OR LOG
*of Land and Sea Tours, &c.*

| DATE. | |
|---|---|
| | |

# JOTTINGS OR LOG
*of Land and Sea Tours, &c.*

| DATE. | |
|-------|---|
| | |

# JOTTINGS OR LOG

*of Land and Sea Tours, &c.*

| DATE. | |
|---|---|
| | |

# JOTTINGS OR LOG
*of Land and Sea Tours, &c.*

| DATE. | |
|-------|--|
| | |

# JOTTINGS OR LOG
*of Land and Sea Tours, &c.*

| DATE. | |
|---|---|
| | |

# JOTTINGS OR LOG
*of Land and Sea Tours, &c.*

| DATE. | |
|---|---|
| | |

# JOTTINGS OR LOG
*of Land and Sea Tours, &c.*

| DATE. | |
|---|---|
| | |

# JOTTINGS OR LOG
*of Land and Sea Tours, &c.*

| DATE. | |
|-------|---|
| | |

# JOTTINGS OR LOG

*of Land and Sea Tours, &c.*

| DATE. | |
|---|---|
| | |

# JOTTINGS OR LOG
*of Land and Sea Tours, &c.*

| DATE. | |
|---|---|
| | |

# JOTTINGS OR LOG
*of Land and Sea Tours, &c.*

| DATE. | |
|-------|--|
|       |  |

# JOTTINGS OR LOG
*of Land and Sea Tours, &c.*

| DATE. | |
|---|---|
| | |

# JOTTINGS OR LOG
*of Land and Sea Tours, &c.*

| DATE. | |
|---|---|
| | |

# JOTTINGS OR LOG
*of Land and Sea Tours, &c.*

| DATE. | |
|---|---|
| | |

# FOREIGN MONEY, &c.

*(Compiled for Bradshaw's Diary.)*

Circular notes are issued by most of the principal London Bankers, and form a very safe and convenient kind of letters of credit. The arrangements for cashing them in the various countries through which the traveller may have to pass, are very simple and efficient, precluding almost the possibility of fraud. A letter indicating the names of the various correspondents abroad, accompanies them, which must be produced on presenting a note for payment, and we should advise tourists, as a precaution, to keep the letter always separate from the notes.

The most advantageous money for travellers proceeding to Germany are Thaler or Florin Notes, according as their destination is for the North or South. *Napoleons* circulate all through Europe, without difficulty, and are the best coin travellers can take; they can invariably be obtained in London at 16s., or sometimes less. Five franc pieces, Prussian dollars, and florins are the most serviceable silver coins. It is scarcely necessary to hint at the advantage of being always provided with small change in the legal current coin of the country through which the traveller passes, as every exchange entails a consequent loss.

## GOLD AND SILVER COIN TABLE,

Shewing the value obtainable for the following Gold and Silver Coins in different Continental countries. Subject to the fluctuations of the Rates of Exchange—for which, see *Bradshaw's Continental Guides*, published on the first of every month.

**The Currency of Switzerland, Italy, France, and Belgium, are the same.**

| DESCRIPTION OF COIN. | Value in English Money. | | | FRANCE, BELGI'M SWITZ'LD | | PRUSSIA. | | | AUSTRIA in Notes | | GERMANY. | | HOLLAND. | | HAMBURGH. | |
|---|---|---|---|---|---|---|---|---|---|---|---|---|---|---|---|---|
| GOLD COIN. | £ | s. | d. | Fr. | Cts. | Thl. | Sgr. | Pf. | Fl. | Cts. | Fl. | Kr. | Gld. | Ct. | Mc. | Shs. |
| English Sovereign | 1 | 0 | 0 | 25 | 15 | 6 | 22 | 6 | 12 | 30 | 12 | 0 | 11 | 95 | 13 | 1 |
| Dutch Ten Florin... | 1 | 16 | 5 | 20 | 85 | 5 | 16 | 6 | 19 | 25 | 9 | 51 | 10 | 0 | 10 | 12 |
| Napoleon............ | 0 | 15 | 10 | 20 | 0 | 5 | 12 | 0 | 9 | 84 | 9 | 36 | 9 | 55 | 10 | 9 |
| Friedrichs d'or | 0 | 16 | 7 | 20 | 85 | 5 | 19 | 6 | 10 | 25 | 9 | 57 | 9 | 96 | 10 | 10½ |
| Louis d'or .......... | 0 | 16 | 4 | 20 | 53 | 5 | 16 | 3 | 10 | 20 | 9 | 48 | 9 | 76 | 10 | 11¼ |
| Ducat (Austrian) ... | 0 | 9 | 4 | 11 | 75 | 3 | 6 | 3 | 5 | 80 | 5 | 36 | 5 | 65 | 6 | 1½ |
| Ducat (Dutch) ...... | 0 | 9 | 3 | 11 | 73 | 3 | 4 | 6 | 5 | 75 | 5 | 33 | 5 | 60 | 6 | 0¾ |
| Eagle ................ | 1 | 0 | 5 | 25 | 65 | 6 | 27 | 6 | 12 | 57½ | 12 | 15 | 12 | 20 | 13 | 5 |
| Half Imperial (Rus.) | 0 | 16 | 3 | 25 | 50 | 5 | 15 | 6 | 10 | 5 | 9 | 45 | 9 | 75 | 10 | 10½ |
| Ten Florin Piece (German) ... | 0 | 16 | 8 | 20 | 95 | 5 | 18 | 9 | 10 | 25 | 10 | 0 | 9 | 96 | 10 | 14½ |
| German Gold Crown | 1 | 7 | 3 | 34 | 37 | 9 | 7 | 6 | 16 | 86 | 16 | 25 | 16 | 40 | 17 | 13½ |
| Isabella (5 dollar) (Spanish) ... | 1 | 0 | 5 | 25 | 67½ | 6 | 27 | 6 | 12 | 65¼ | 12 | 15 | 12 | 25 | 13 | 5 |
| SILVER COIN. | | | | | | | | | | | | | | | | |
| English Shilling ... | 0 | 1 | 0 | 1 | 25 | 0 | 10 | 1½ | 0 | 61½ | 0 | 36 | 0 | 60 | 0 | 10½ |
| Five Franc Piece ... | 0 | 3 | 11 | 5 | 0 | 1 | 10 | 6 | 2 | 46 | 2 | 24 | 2 | 39 | 2 | 10 |
| One Franc Piece ... | 0 | 0 | 9 | 1 | 0 | 0 | 8 | 0 | 0 | 48 | 0 | 28 | 0 | 47½ | 0 | |
| Thaler (Prussian)... | 0 | 2 | 11 | 3 | 75 | 1 | 0 | 0 | 1 | 84 | 1 | 49 | 1 | 69½ | 2 | 0 |
| Florin (German) / Florin (Dutch) ... | 0 | 1 | 8 | 2 | 10 | 0 | 16 | 10½ | 1 | 2⅜ | 1 | 0 | 1 | 0 | 1 | 1½ |
| Florin (Austrian ... | 0 | 1 | 11 | 2 | 50 | 0 | 20 | 0 | 1 | 22 | 1 | 12 | 1 | 19½ | 1 | 4¾ |
| American Dollar ... | 0 | 4 | 0 | 5 | 0 | 1 | 10 | 0 | 2 | 46 | 2 | 24 | 2 | 37 | 2 | 10 |

# A CONCISE TABLE OF FOREIGN MONIES.

## REDUCED FROM ENGLISH MONEY INTO THE CURRENCY OF OTHER COUNTRIES.

| ENGLAND. | FRANCE, BELGIUM, SWITZ'LD | PRUSSIA. | AUSTRIA, in Notes. | HOLLAND | GERMANY | RUSSIA, in Paper. | HAMBURGH. |
|---|---|---|---|---|---|---|---|
| £ s. d. | Frs. Cts. | Th. Sgr. Pf. | Fl. Cts. | Fl. Cts. | Fl. Kr. | Rbl. Kop | Marc. Sch |
| 0 0 0¼ | 0 2½ | 0 0 2½ | 0 1¼ | 0 1¼ | 0 0¾ | 0 0¾ | 0 0¼ |
| 0 0 0½ | 0 5¼ | 0 0 5 | 0 2½ | 0 2½ | 0 1½ | 0 1½ | 0 0½ |
| 0 0 0¾ | 0 7¾ | 0 0 7½ | 0 3¾ | 0 3¾ | 0 2¼ | 0 2¼ | 0 0¾ |
| 0 0 1 | 0 10½ | 0 0 10 | 0 5 | 0 5 | 0 3 | 0 3 | 0 1 |
| 0 0 2 | 0 21 | 0 1 8 | 0 10½ | 0 0 | 0 6 | 0 6¼ | 0 1¾ |
| 0 0 3 | 0 31 | 0 2 6½ | 0 15¼ | 0 5 | 0 9 | 0 9½ | 0 2¾ |
| 0 0 4 | 0 42 | 0 3 4½ | 0 20½ | 0 0 | 0 12 | 0 12½ | 0 3¾ |
| 0 0 5 | 0 52 | 0 4 2½ | 0 25½ | 0 5 | 0 15 | 0 15¾ | 0 4 |
| 0 0 6 | 0 63 | 0 5 0¾ | 0 30¾ | 0 30 | 0 18 | 0 18¾ | 0 5¼ |
| 0 0 7 | 0 73 | 0 5 10¾ | 0 35¾ | 0 35 | 0 21 | 0 22 | 0 6 |
| 0 0 8 | 0 84 | 0 6 9 | 0 41 | 0 40 | 0 24 | 0 25 | 0 6¾ |
| 0 0 9 | 0 94 | 0 7 7 | 0 46 | 6 45 | 0 27 | 0 28¼ | 0 8 |
| 0 0 10 | 1 5 | 0 8 6 | 0 51¼ | 0 50 | 0 36 | 0 31¼ | 0 8¾ |
| 0 0 11 | 1 15 | 0 9 3¼ | 0 56¼ | 0 55 | 0 33 | 0 34½ | 0 9½ |
| 0 1 0 | 1 26 | 0 10 1½ | 0 61½ | 0 59¾ | 0 36 | 0 37½ | 0 10½ |
| 0 2 0 | 2 52 | 0 20 3 | 1 23 | 1 19½ | 1 12 | 0 75 | 1 5 |
| 0 3 0 | 3 77 | 1 0 4½ | 1 84½ | 1 79½ | 1 48 | 1 12½ | 2 0 |
| 0 4 0 | 5 3 | 1 10 6 | 2 46 | 2 39 | 2 24 | 1 50 | 2 10 |
| 0 5 0 | 6 26 | 1 20 7½ | 3 7½ | 2 98½ | 3 0 | 1 87½ | 3 4½ |
| 0 6 0 | 7 55 | 2 0 9 | 3 69 | 3 58½ | 3 36 | 2 25 | 3 15 |
| 0 7 0 | 8 80 | 2 10 10½ | 4 30½ | 4 18¼ | 4 12 | 2 62½ | 4 10 |
| 0 8 0 | 10 6 | 2 21 0 | 4 92 | 4 78 | 4 48 | 3 0 | 5 4 |
| 0 9 0 | 11 32 | 3 1 1½ | 5 53½ | 5 37¾ | 5 24 | 3 37½ | 5 14¼ |
| 0 10 0 | 12 58 | 3 11 3 | 6 15 | 5 97½ | 6 0 | 3 75 | 6 8½ |
| 0 11 0 | 13 83 | 3 21 4½ | 6 76½ | 6 57¼ | 6 36 | 4 12½ | 7 3¼ |
| 0 12 0 | 15 9 | 4 1 6 | 7 38 | 7 17 | 7 12 | 4 50 | 7 14 |
| 0 13 0 | 16 35 | 4 11 7½ | 7 99½ | 7 76¾ | 7 48 | 4 87½ | 8 8½ |
| 0 14 0 | 17 61 | 4 21 9 | 8 61 | 8 36½ | 8 24 | 5 25 | 9 4 |
| 0 15 0 | 19 40 | 5 1 10½ | 9 22½ | 8 96¼ | 9 0 | 4 62½ | 9 14¾ |
| 0 16 0 | 20 12 | 5 12 0 | 9 84 | 9 56 | 9 36 | 6 0 | 10 8 |
| 0 17 0 | 21 38 | 5 22 1½ | 10 45½ | 10 15¾ | 10 12 | 6 37½ | 11 2½ |
| 0 18 0 | 22 63 | 6 2 3 | 11 7 | 10 75½ | 10 48 | 6 75 | 11 12¾ |
| 0 19 0 | 23 89 | 6 12 4½ | 11 68½ | 11 35¼ | 11 24 | 7 12½ | 12 6¾ |
| 1 0 0 | 25 15 | 6 22 6 | 12 30 | 11 95 | 12 0 | 7 50 | 13 1 |
| 2 0 0 | 50 13 | 13 15 0 | 24 60 | 23 90 | 24 0 | 15 0 | 26 2 |
| 3 0 0 | 75 45 | 20 7 6 | 36 90 | 35 85 | 36 0 | 22 50 | 39 3 |
| 4 0 0 | 100 60 | 27 0 0 | 49 20 | 47 80 | 48 0 | 30 0 | 52 4 |
| 5 0 0 | 125 75 | 33 22 6 | 61 50 | 59 75 | 60 0 | 37 50 | 66 5 |
| 6 0 0 | 150 90 | 40 15 0 | 73 80 | 71 70 | 72 0 | 45 0 | 78 6 |
| 7 0 0 | 176 5 | 47 7 6 | 86 10 | 83 65 | 84 0 | 52 50 | 91 7 |
| 8 0 0 | 201 20 | 54 0 0 | 98 40 | 95 60 | 96 0 | 60 0 | 104 8 |
| 9 0 0 | 226 25 | 60 22 6 | 110 70 | 107 55 | 108 0 | 67 50 | 117 9 |
| 10 0 0 | 251 60 | 67 15 0 | 123 0 | 119 50 | 120 0 | 75 0 | 130 10 |

**Austrian Notes.**—The Austrian Paper Currency is at present subject to great fluctuation; owing to the disturbed state of political affairs and the late war, a very serious depreciation has taken place. The present value of the £1 is 12fl. 30c., or about 1s. 7½d. per florin.

### EXPLANATION OF THE CURRENCIES OF THE VARIOUS COUNTRIES.

| | | English Value. s. d. |
|---|---|---|
| **France, Belgium, Switzerland, or Italy** | 1 franc = 100 centimes | = 0 9½ |
| **Prussia, Saxony, Hanover, and North Germany** | 1 thaler = 30 Silver Groschen | = 2 11 |
| **Baden, Bavaria, South Germany** | 1 florin = 60 kreutzers | = 1 8 |
| **Austria** | 1 „ = 100 cents | = 1 11½ |
| **Holland** | 1 florin = 100 cents | = 1s. 8d. |
| **Hamburg** | 1 Mark Courant = 16 Shil. | = 1 1½ |
| **Russia** | 1 Sil. Rouble = 100 Kopecks. | = 3 2 |
| **Spain** | 1 Dollar = 20 Reals | = 4 2 |
| **Portugal** | 1 Milrea = 1000 Reis | = 4 5½ |
| **Greece** | 1 Drachma = 100 Leptas | = 0 8½ |
| **America** | 1 Dollar = 100 Cents | = 4 0 |

**Russia.**—It must not be forgotten that the Currency in Russia represented by Rouble Notes, has of late years seriously depreciated, the Paper Rouble being worth 32 pence, whereas the Silver Rouble is worth 37 to 37½ pence.

# ENGLISH CURRENCY.

*(Compiled for Bradshaw's Diary from Dietrichsen and Hannay's Almanack, &c.)*

## GOLD COIN.

The standard gold coin of England is made of a metal consisting of 22 parts of pure gold, and 2 parts of copper. The pound sterling is represented by a gold coin called a sovereign, and from a pound troy of gold, are coined $46\frac{39}{40}$ sovereigns, so that the weight of each is exactly 5 dwts. $3\frac{171}{623}$ grs., or nearly 123·274 grs.; and the Mint price of standard gold is £3 17s. 10½d. per ounce.

## SILVER COIN.

The standard silver coin consists of 37 parts of pure silver and 3 parts of copper; and a pound troy of this metal furnishes 66 shillings, so that the weight of a shilling is 3 dwts. $13\frac{3}{11}$ grs.; and the Mint price of standard silver is 5s. 6d per ounce. The silver coinage is not a legal tender for more than 40s., the gold coinage above mentioned being the only general standard of value.

In the copper coinage, 24 pence are made from an avoirdupoise pound of copper, so that a penny should weigh 10 drs. avoirdupois, or $291\frac{2}{3}$ grs. troy; but this is not a legal tender for more than 12d.

*Note.*—This copper coinage is now superseded by a metal coinage of less intrinsic value.

A Farthing is written or marked ¼d.

| | | | |
|---|---|---|---|
| 2 Farthings are 1 Halfpenny ............... ½d. | 12 Pence are 1 Shilling ............ ............ 1s. |
| 4 Farthings are 1 Penny ..................... 1d. | 20 Shillings, 1 pound, or a sovereign ......£1 |

A Farthing is the lowest denomination in use, but it is customary to denote farthings by fractions of a penny as in the table.

Money as expressed by means of these denominations is commonly called sterling money, in order to distinguish it from stock, &c., which is merely nominal.

Though all commercial transactions are conducted by means of the money enumerated in the preceding table, there are other coins or denominations frequently met with, and some of them more particularly in old documents, of which the following are the most important, and their values in currents money is here annexed:—

| | £ s. d. | | £ s. d. | | £ s. d. |
|---|---|---|---|---|---|
| A Threepenny is......| 0 0 3 | A Seven Shilling Piece | 0 7 0 | A Mark................| 0 13 4 |
| A Groat or Fourpenny | 0 0 4 | A Half Sovereign ...... | 0 10 0 | A Carolus ............ | 1 3 0 |
| A Tester................... | 0 0 6 | A Half Guinea........... | 0 10 6 | A Jacobus............ | 1 5 0 |
| A Florin................... | 0 2 0 | A Guinea ................. | 1 1 0 | A Moidore ........ | 1 5 0 |
| A Half Crown ......... | 0 2 6 | A Noble..................... | 0 6 8 | A Six and Thirty... | 1 16 0 |
| A Crown .............. | 0 5 0 | An Angel ................... | 0 10 0 | | |

## STANDARD OF GOLD FOR MANUFACTURED ARTICLES.

By an Order in Council in pursuance of 17 and 18 Vict. cap. xcvi., any Gold Vessel, Plate, or Manufacture of Gold may be wrought of any of the following standards, viz:—1st. The standard of 15 carats fine gold in every pound Troy.—2nd. The standard of 12 carats in every pound Troy.—3rd. The standard of 9 carats in every pound Troy.

## WEIGHT OF ENGLISH COINS.

| GOLD. | dwt. | gr. | SILVER. | dwt. | gr. |
|---|---|---|---|---|---|
| Sovereign..................... | 5 | 3¼ | Half Crown ................. | 9 | 2 2-11 |
| Half Sovereign ............ | 2 | 13½ | Florin............................ | 7 | 6 6-11 |
| Double Sovereign ......... | 10 | 6½ | Shilling ........................ | 3 | 15 3-11 |
| SILVER. | | | Sixpence ...................... | 1 | 19 7-11 |
| Crown ...................... | 18 | 4 4-11 | Fourpence..................... | 1 | 5 1-11 |

## CURRENCY OF THE UNITED KINGDOM.

*Compiled for Bradshaw's Diary from British Statistical Register.*

| | | | |
|---|---|---|---|
| Sovereign ......................| £68,000,000 | Silver Coin ..................... | £14,000,000 |
| Half Sovereign.................. | 12,000,000 | Copper .......................... | 1,000,000 |
| Total .................. | | | 95,000,000 |

## CIRCULATING MEDIUM OF THE UNITED KINGDOM.

| | | | |
|---|---|---|---|
| Coin ...................................... | £95,000,000 | English Bank Notes ............ | £3,500,000 |
| Bullion.................................... | 15,000,000 | Scotch and Irish Notes ......... | 5,500,000 |
| Notes used by Bank of England for Security .................. | 15,000,000 | Total.......................... | £134,000,000 |

# ENGLISH WEIGHTS, MEASURES, &c.

*(Compiled and arranged for Bradshaw's Diary.)*

## 1. MEASURE OF LENGTH.

| | | |
|---|---|---|
| 12 | Inches | = 1 Foot |
| 3 | Feet | = 1 Yard |
| 5½ | Yards | = { 1 Rod, Pole, or Perch |
| 40 | Poles or 220 Yards | = 1 Furlong |
| 8 | Furlongs or 1,760 ,, | = 1 Mile |
| 3 | Miles or 5,280 ,, | = 1 League |
| 60 | Geographical Miles or 69½ English Miles | = { 1 Degree of a Great Circle of the Earth |

An inch is the smallest lineal measure to which a name is given, but subdivisions are used for many purposes. Among mechanics, the inch is commonly divided into *eighths*. By the officers of the revenue, and by scientific persons, it is divided into *tenths, hundredths,* &c.

### *Particular Measures of Length.*

| | | | |
|---|---|---|---|
| A Nail | = 2¼ Inches | | used for measuring cloth of all kinds. |
| Quarter | = 4 Nails | | |
| Yard | = 4 Quarters | | |
| Ell | = 5 Quarters | | |
| Hand | = 4 Inches | | used for height of horses. |
| Span | = 9 Inches | | used in measuring depths. |
| Fathom | = 6 Feet | | |
| Pace (Military) | = 2½ Feet | | |
| Pace (Geometrical) | = 5 Feet | | |
| Link | = { 7 Inches 92 hdths. | | used in Land Measure to facilitate computation of the content, 10 square chains being equal to an acre. |
| Chain | = { 4 Poles or 22 Yards | | |
| | 100 Links | | |

## 2. MEASURE OF SURFACE.

| | | | |
|---|---|---|---|
| 144 | Sq. Inches | = | 1 Sq. Foot |
| 9 | Sq. Feet | = | 1 Sq. Yard |
| 30¼ | Sq. Yards | = | 1 Perch or Rod |
| 40 | Sq. Perches | = | 1 Rood |
| 4 | Sq. Roods | = | 1 Acre |
| 640 | Sq. Acres | = | 1 Sq. Mile |

## 3. MEASURES OF SOLIDITY AND CAPACITY.

### DIVISION I.—SOLIDITY.

| | | |
|---|---|---|
| 1728 Cubic Inches | = | 1 Cubic Foot |
| 27 Cubic Feet | = | 1 Cubic Yard |

### DIVISION II.—CAPACITY.

| | | |
|---|---|---|
| 4 Gills or Noggins | = | 1 Pint |
| 2 Pints | = | 1 Quart |
| 2 Quarts | = | 1 Pottle |
| 4 Quarts | = | 1 Gallon |
| 2 Pottles or ½ a Peck | = | 1 Gallon |
| 2 Gallons | = | 1 Peck |
| 8 Gallons | = | 1 Bushel |
| 4 Pecks | = | 1 Bushel |
| 3 Bushels | = | 1 Sack |
| 8 Bushels | = | 1 Quarter |
| 12 Sacks | = | 1 Chaldron |
| 5 Quarters | = | 1 Load |

The four last denominations are used for dry goods only. For liquids several denominations have been heretofore adopted, viz.:— For Beer, the Firkin of 9 Gallons, the Kilderkin of 18, the Barrel of 36, the Hogshead of 54, and the Butt of 108 Gallons. Flour is sold nominally by measure, but actually by weight, reckoned at 7 lbs. avoirdupois to a gallon.

## 4. MEASURE OF WEIGHT.

### DIVISION I.—AVOIRDUPOIS WEIGHT.

| | | |
|---|---|---|
| 27 11/32 Grains | = 1 Drachm | = 27 11/32 gr. |
| 16 Drachms | = 1 Ounce | = 437½ — |
| 16 Ounces | = 1 Pound (lb.) | = 7000 |
| 28 Pounds or 2 Stone | = 1 Quarter (qr.) | |
| 8 Stone | = 1 cwt. | |
| 4 Quarters | = 1 Hundredweight (cwt.) | |
| 20 Cwt. | = 1 Ton | |

This weight is used in almost all commercial transactions, and for nearly all the necessaries and common dealings of life.

The particular weights belonging to this Division are as follow:—cwt., qr., lb.

| | | cwt. | qr. | lb. | |
|---|---|---|---|---|---|
| 14 Pounds | = 1 Stone | = 0 | 0 | 14 | |
| 2 Stone | = 1 Tod | = 0 | 1 | 0 | Used in the wool trade. |
| 6½ Tod | = 1 Wey | = 1 | 2 | 14 | |
| 2 Weys | = 1 Sack | = 3 | 1 | 0 | |
| 12 Sacks | = 1 Last | = 39 | 0 | 0 | |

### DIVISION II.—TROY WEIGHT.

| | | |
|---|---|---|
| 24 Grains | = 1 Pennyweight | = 24 gr. |
| 20 Pennyweights | = 1 Ounce | = 480 — |
| 12 Ounces | = 1 Pound | = 5760 — |

These are the denominations of Troy Weight when used for weighing gold, silver, and precious stones (except diamonds). But Troy Weight is also used by Apothecaries in compounding medicines, and by them the ounce is divided into 8 drams, and the dram into 3 scruples, so that the scruple is equal to 20 grains.

For scientific purposes the grain only is used; and sets of weights are constructed in decimal progression, from 10,000 grains downwards to 1-100th of a grain.

The *carat*, used for weighing diamonds, is 3 1-6th grains. The term, however, when used to express the fineness of gold, has a relative meaning only. Every mass of alloyed gold is supposed to be divided into 24 equal parts; thus the standard for coin is 22 carats fine. that is, it consists of 22 parts of pure gold and 2 parts of alloy.

## 5. ANGULAR MEASURE;

### OR, DIVISIONS OF THE CIRCLE.

| | |
|---|---|
| 60 Seconds | = 1 Minute |
| 60 Minutes | = 1 Degree |
| 30 Degrees | = 1 Sign |
| 90 Degrees | = 1 Quadrant |
| 360 Degrees, or 12 Signs | = 1 Circumference |

## 6. MEASURE OF TIME.

| | |
|---|---|
| 60 Seconds | = 1 Minute |
| 60 Minutes | = 1 Hour |
| 24 Hours | = 1 Day |
| 7 Days | = 1 Week |
| 28 Days | = 1 Lunar Month |
| 28, 29, 30, or 31 Days | = 1 Calendar Month |
| 12 Calendar Months | = 1 Year |
| 365 Days | = 1 Common Year |
| 366 Days | = 1 Leap Year |

In 400 years, 97 are leap years, and 303 common.

# MISCELLANEOUS.

|  | | | | lb. | oz. |
|---|---|---|---|---|---|
| A peck loaf weighs | ... | ... | ... | ... | 17 | 6½ |
| A half-peck loaf... | ... | ... | ... | ... | 8 | 11 |
| A quartern loaf | ... | ... | ... | ... | 4 | 5 |

| | lbs. | | lbs. |
|---|---|---|---|
| A firkin of butter is ... ... | 56 | Bushel of coal ... ... | 64 |
| —— in Ireland ... | 80 to 84 | Hundredweight of potatoes ... | 120 |
| —— soap ... ... | 64 | Ton of potatoes ... | 40 bushels |
| Barrel of anchovies ... ... | 30 | Thousand of quills ... | ... 1200 |
| —— butter ... ... | 224 | Hundred of walnuts ... | ... 120 |
| —— candles ... ... | 120 | Paper, a quire ... | 24 sheets |
| Fother of lead ... ... | 218½ | —— a ream ... | 20 quires |
| Gallon of train oil ... ... | 7½ | —— a bundle ... | 2 reams |
| Stone of iron or shot ... ... | 14 | Load of hay or straw... | 36 trusses |
| —— glass ... ... | 5 | Truss of straw ... | 36 lbs. |
| —— meat (London) ... | 8 | —— old hay ... | 56 „ |
| —— (country) ... | 14 | —— new hay ... | 60 „ |
| —— cheese ... ... | 16 | A pipe of Port   115 imperial gallons |
| —— hemp ... ... | 32 | —— Cape or Madeira 92   „      „ |
| —— fish ... ... | 8 | A butt of Sherry    103   „      „ |
| Gallon of flour ... ... | 7 | A hogshead of Claret  46   „      „ |

A standard gallon contains 10 lbs. avoirdupois of distilled water.

A weigh of cheese, 256 lbs.

Herrings are measured by the barrel of 26⅝ or cran of 37½ gallons.

| Flour, peck or stone ... | ... | ... | ... | 14 | pounds. |
|---|---|---|---|---|---|
| —— bushel | ... | ... | ... | 56 | „ |
| —— boll of 10 pecks or stones ... | ... | ... | 140 | „ |
| —— sack of 2 bolls or 5 bushels | ... | ... | 280 | „ |
| —— barrel | ... | ... | ... | 196 | „ |

Oranges, lemons, corks, and a few other articles, are often sold by the gross; nails, tacks, &c., have six score to the hundred.

An imperial gallon of whale or seal oil should weigh 9 lbs., or sperm oil, 8 lbs. 10 ounces.

A pocket of hops, average weight about 1½ cwt. to 2 cwt.

| | | | | | | lbs. |
|---|---|---|---|---|---|---|
| A peck of potatoes | ... | ... | ... | ... | ... | 20 |
| —— white turnips | ... | ... | ... | ... | ... | 16 |
| —— Swede turnips | ... | ... | ... | ... | ... | 18 |
| —— onions | ... | ... | ... | ... | ... | 16 |
| —— broad beans | ... | ... | ... | ... | ... | 10 |
| —— kidney beans | ... | ... | ... | ... | ... | 9 |
| —— green peas | ... | ... | ... | ... | ... | 9 |
| —— apples ... | ... | ... | ... | ... | ... | 16 |
| —— pears ... | ... | ... | ... | ... | ... | 18 |
| —— gooseberries | ... | ... | ... | ... | ... | 16 |
| —— plums, damsons, and all stone fruit ... | ... | ... | 18 |

## FRENCH WEIGHTS AND MEASURES.

Their *Metre* is 39¼ English inches—their *Hectare* is 2·47 acres, the *Are* ($\frac{1}{100}$ of Hectare) about 4 perches—the *Litre* is 0·22 gallon, the *Hectolitre* (100 Litres) 22·8 gallons—the *Kilogramme* 2·205 lbs. av. (*See* French Weights and Measures, pages 59 60.)

# FRENCH WEIGHTS AND MEASURES, &c.

*(Compiled for Bradshaw's Diary, from Weale's Rudimentary Series of Weights and Measures).*

---

## 1. METRICAL SYSTEM NOW IN USE.

### Length.

| | ENGLISH VALUE. |
|---|---|
| Millimètre (1000th of a mètre) | 0·03937 inches. |
| Centimètre (100th of a mètre) | 0·39371 ,, |
| Décimètre (10th of a mètre) | 3·93708 ,, |
| Mètre (unit of length) | 39·3708 ,, or 3·2809 feet. |
| Décamètre (10 mètres) | 32·809 feet. 10·9363 yards. |
| Hectomètre (100 mètres) | 328·09 ,, 109·3633 ,, |
| Kilomètre (1000 mètres) | 1093·63 yards or 0·62138 miles. |
| Myriamètre (10,000 mètres) | 10936·33 ,, 6·21382 ,, |

### Surface.

| | |
|---|---|
| Centiare { (100th of an are or a square metre) | 1·1960 square yards. |
| Are { (square décamètre and unit of surface) | 119·6033 ,, ,, or 0·0247 acres. |
| Decare (10 ares) | 1196·033 ,, ,, 0·2474 ,, |
| Hectare (100 ares) | 11960·33 ,, ,, 2·4736 ,, |

### Capacity.

| | |
|---|---|
| Millitre { (1000th of a litre or cubic centimetre) | 0·06103 cubic inches. |
| Centilitre (100th of a litre) | 0·61027 ,, ,, |
| Decilitre (18th of a litre) | 9·10270 ,, ,, |
| Litre { (cubic decimetre and unit of capacity) | 61·02705 ,, ,, or 1·7608 pints. |
| Decalitre (10 litres) | 610·2705 ,, ,, 2·2010 gallons. |
| Hectolitre (100 litres) | 3·53166 cubic feet 22·0097 ,, |
| Kilolitre { (1000 litres or cubic metre) | 35·31658 ,, ,, 220·0967 ,, |
| Myrialitre (10,000 litres) | 353·1658 ,, ,, 2200·9667 ,, |

### Solid.

| | |
|---|---|
| Décistere (10th of a stère) | 3·5317 cubic feet. |
| Stère (cubic metre) | 35·3166 ,, ,, |
| Décastère (10 stères) | 353·1658 ,, ,, |

## *Weight.*

ENGLISH VALUE.

| | |
|---|---|
| Milligramme (1000th of a gramme) | 0·0154 grains. |
| Centigramme (100th of a gramme) | 0·1544 ,, |
| Decigramme (10th of a gramme) | 1·5440 ,, |
| Gramme (unit of weight) | 15·44 ,, |
| Decagramme (10 grammes) | 154·4 ,, |
| Hectogramme (100 grammes) | 1544 grains $\begin{cases} 3\cdot2167 \text{ oz. troy, or} \\ 3\cdot5291 \text{ oz. avoirdupois.} \end{cases}$ |
| Kilogramme (1000 grammes) | 32⅙ oz. troy or 2·2057 lbs. ,, |
| Myriagramme (10,000 grammes) | 132¾ ,, 22·057 ,, ,, |

## 2. "SYSTEME USUEL."

(Formerly in use, but interdicted since 1840.)

### *Length.*

| | |
|---|---|
| 12 lignes make 1 pouce | 1·094 inches. |
| 12 pouces ,, 1 "pied usuel" | 13·124 ,, or 1·0936 feet. |
| 3 pieds ,, 1 metre | 39·371 ,, 3·2809 ,, |
| 2 metres ,, 1 toise | 78·742 ,, 6·5618 ,, |
| The aune is $\begin{cases} 12 \text{ decimetres} \\ 1\frac{1}{5} \text{ metre} \end{cases}$ | 47·245 ,, 3·9371 ,, |

### *Weight.*

| | |
|---|---|
| 72 grains make 1 gros | 60·31 grains troy. |
| 8 gros ,, 1 once | 482·5 ,, = 1·0052 oz. troy. |
| 8 onces ,, 1 mark | 3860 ,, = 8·0417 ,, |
| 2 marks ,, 1 livre = 500 grammes $\}$ | 7720 ,, $\begin{cases} = 1\cdot3403 \text{ lb. troy,} \\ \text{or } 1\cdot1029 \text{ ,, avoird.} \end{cases}$ |

## 3. ANCIENT SYSTEM.

### *Length.*

| | |
|---|---|
| 12 lignes make 1 pouce or inch | 1·066 inches. |
| 12 pouces $\begin{cases} \text{,, 1 "pied de Roi"} \\ (0\cdot3249 \text{ metre}) \end{cases}$ | 12·79 ,, |
| 6 pieds ,, 1 toise (1·9492 ,, | 6·395 feet. |
| The aune (1·1880 ,, | 46·85 inches. |
| "Lieue de poste" (2000 toises) | 4263 yards or 2·4222 miles. |

### *Weight.*

| | |
|---|---|
| 72 grains make 1 gros | 59·0 grains troy. |
| 8 gros ,, 1 once | 472·2 ,, ,, = 0·9837 oz. troy. |
| 8 onces ,, 1 mark | 3777·5 ,, ,, = 7·8698 ,, |
| 2 marks ,, 1 poids de marc | 7555 ,, $\begin{cases} 1\cdot3116 \text{ lb. troy, or} \\ 1\cdot0793 \text{ ,, avoird.} \end{cases}$ |

# DISTANCES OR ROAD MEASURES OF PRINCIPAL COUNTRIES IN THE WORLD.

*(Compiled for Bradshaw's Diary from Weale's Rudimentary Series of Weights and Measures.)*

| COUNTRY. | DISTANCE. | Equal to Engl. Yds. |
|---|---|---|
| Arabia | Mile | 2,146 |
| Austria | Mile or post (24,000 Vienna feet) | 8,297 |
| Do. | Mile—Marine—60 to degree | 2,025 |
| Baden | Mile | 9,721 |
| Bavaria | Mile | 8,059 |
| Belgium | Mile (old measure) | 2,132 |
| Do. | Mile—Marine—63 to degree | 2,025 |
| Do. | Mile—Metrical—Kilometre | 1,094 |
| Brazil | League—18 to degree | 6,751 |
| Bremen | Mile | 6,865 |
| Brunswick | Mile | 11,816 |
| China | Li or Mile | 609 |
| Denmark | Mile | 8,238 |
| England | Mile—Statute | 1,760 |
| Do. | Mile—Geographical—60 to degree | 2,025 |
| Do. | League—Geographical—20 to degree | 6,076 |
| France | Mile (old measure) | 2,132 |
| Do. | Mile—Marine—60 to degree | 2,025 |
| Do. | Mile—Metrical—Kilometre | 1,094 |
| Germany | Mile—Geographical—15 to degree | 8,101 |
| Do. | Mile—Long Geographical—12 to degree | 10,126 |
| Do. | Mile—Short | 6,859 |
| Greece | Mile | 1,640 |
| Hamburg | Mile | 8,238 |
| Hanover | Mile | 7,442 |
| Hebrew | Ancient Eastern Mile of 4,000 Cubits | 2,432 |
| Holland | Mile (old measure) | 6,396 |
| Do. | Mile—Marine | 6,076 |
| Do. | Mile—Legal | 1,094 |
| Hungary | Mile or League | 9,002 |
| India | Bengal Coss or mile | 2,000 |
| Do. | League—30 to degree | 4,051 |
| Do. | Do.   Carnatic—35 to degree | 3,472 |
| Italy | Mile—60 to degree | 2,025 |
| Norway | Mile | 12,182 |
| Persia | Parasang | 6,076 |
| Poland | League—Long | 8,101 |
| Portugal | Mile | 2,250 |
| Do. | Mile—Marine | 2,025 |
| Prussia | Mile—24,000 Rhineland feet | 8,238 |
| Do. | Mile—Geographical—15 to degree | 8,101 |
| Rome | Mile—74¼ to degree | 1,630 |
| Do. | Mile—Metrical—Kilometre | 1,094 |
| Russia | Werst or Verst | 1,167 |
| Saxony | Mile-post | 7,432 |
| Spain | Mile | 1,522 |
| Do. | Mile—Marine— 60 to degree | 2,025 |
| Sweden | Mile | 11,690 |
| Switzerland | Mile | 8,548 |
| Turkey | Verri—66¼ to degree | 1,827 |
| United States | Mile | 1,760 |

# The POPULATION of the different Counties of ENGLAND and WALES in 1861.

| COUNTY. | Population. | COUNTY. | Population. |
|---|---|---|---|
| Bedford ... ... ... ... ... ... | 135,265 | Rutland ... ... ... ... ... | 21,859 |
| Berks ... ... ... ... ... ... | 176,163 | Salop ... ... ... ... ... | 240,876 |
| Buckingham... ... ... ... ... | 166,597 | Somerset ... ... ... ... ... | 444,725 |
| Cambridge ... ... ... ... ... | 175,950 | Southampton ... ... ... ... | 481,495 |
| Chester ... ... ... ... ... | 505,153 | Stafford ... ... ... ... ... | 746,584 |
| Cornwall ... ... ... ... ... | 369,323 | Suffolk ... ... ... ... ... | 336,271 |
| Cumberland ... ... ... ... ... | 205,293 | Surrey ... ... ... ... ... | 831,685 |
| Derby ... ... ... ... ... ... | 339,377 | Sussex ... ... ... ... ... | 363,648 |
| Devon ... ... ... ... ... ... | 584,531 | Warwick ... ... ... ... | 561,728 |
| Dorset ... ... ... ... ... ... | 188,651 | Westmorland ... ... ... | 60,809 |
| Durham ... ... ... ... ... ... | 509,018 | Wilts ... ... ... ... ... | 249,455 |
| Essex ... ... ... ... ... ... | 404,644 | Worcester ... ... ... ... | 307,601 |
| Gloucester ... ... ... ... ... | 485,502 | York ... ... ... ... ... | 2,033,051 |
| Hereford ... ... ... ... ... | 123,659 | WALES. | |
| Hertford ... ... ... ... ... | 173,294 | | |
| Huntingdon .. ... ... ... ... | 64,207 | Anglesey ... ... ... ... ... | 54,546 |
| Kent ... ... ... ... ... ... | 733,675 | Brecon ... ... ... ... ... | 61,627 |
| Lancaster ... ... ... ... ... | 2,428,744 | Cardigan ... ... ... ... | 72,255 |
| Leicester ... ... ... ... ... | 237,402 | Carmarthen ... ... ... ... | 111,757 |
| Lincoln ... ... ... ... ... | 411,997 | Carnarvon ... ... ... ... | 95,668 |
| Middlesex ... ... ... ... ... | 2,205,771 | Denbigh ... ... ... ... | 100,862 |
| Monmouth ... ... ... ... ... | 174,670 | Flint ... ... ... ... ... | 69,870 |
| Norfolk ... ... ... ... ... .. | 435,422 | Glamorgan ... ... ... ... | 317,751 |
| Northampton ... ... ... ... | 227,727 | Merioneth ... ... ... ... | 38,888 |
| Northumberland ... ... ... ... | 343,028 | Montgomery ... ... ... ... | 67,975 |
| Nottingham ... ... ... ... ... | 293,784 | Pembroke ... ... ... ... | 96,093 |
| Oxford ... ... ... ... ... ... | 172,266 | Radnor... ... ... .. ... | 25,403 |

# POPULATION of some of the Principal Countries in the World.
*(From Martin's Statesman's Year Book.)*

| COUNTRY. | Population. | COUNTRY. | Population. |
|---|---|---|---|
| Austria ... ... ... ... ... ... | 34,670,577 | Italy ... ... ... ... ... ... | 21,703,710 |
| Bavaria ... ... ... ... ... ... | 4,689,837 | Mexico ... ... ... ... ... | 7,995,426 |
| Belgium ... ... ... ... ... ... | 4,984,451 | Persia ... ... ... ... ... | 4,400,000 |
| Brazils ... ... ... ... ... ... | 7,677,800 | Portugal ... ... ... ... ... | 3,987,867 |
| British India ... ... ... ... ... | 135,634,244 | Prussia ... ... ... ... ... | 22,769,436 |
| China ... ... ... ... ... ... | 367,632,907 | Russia ... ... ... ... ... | 73,892,373 |
| Denmark ... ... ... ... ... | 1,608,095 | Spain ... ... ... ... ... | 16,301,850 |
| France ... ... ... ... ... ... | 38,067,094 | Sweden and Norway ... ... | 5,814,386 |
| Germany ... ... ... ... ... | 36,555,599 | Switzerland ... ... ... ... | 2,534,242 |
| Greece ... ... ... ... ... ... | 1,332,508 | Turkey ... ... ... ... ... | 35,350,000 |
| Holland ... ... ... ... ... ... | 3,756,516 | United States ... ... ... | 31,445,089 |

# POPULATION of the United Kingdom—Census 1861. †

| GREAT BRITAIN:— | POPULATION. | | INCREASE IN 1861. | | DECREASE IN 1861. | |
|---|---|---|---|---|---|---|
| | 1861. | 1851. | Persons. | Per cent. | Persons. | Per cent. |
| England and Wales ........ | 20,061,725 | 17,927,609 | 2,134,116 | 12 | ... | ... |
| Scotland ................. | 3,061,117 | 2,888,742 | 172,375 | 6 | ... | ... |
| Ireland ................. | 5,764,543 | 6,552,145 | ... | ... | 787,842 | 12 |
| Islands in the British Seas | 143,779 | 143,126 | 653 | ... | ... | ... |
| Total of the United Kingdom............ } | 29,031,164 | 27,511,862 | 2,307,144 | ... | 787,842 | ... |

Net increase 1,419,302, or 6 per cent.

† This Tabular statement is taken from the census of 1861. It is exclusive of the Army serving abroad and in Ireland, and of the Navy and Merchant Seamen absent at sea.

# IMPORTS AND EXPORTS OF THE PRINCIPAL COUNTRIES OF THE WORLD.

*(Compiled and Arranged from " Martin's Stateman's Year Book, 1869.")*

| COUNTRY. | Total Imports. | Total Exports. | Trade of each Country with the United Kingdom. | |
| --- | --- | --- | --- | --- |
| | | | Imports from United Kingdom. | Exports to the United Kingdom. |
| | £ | £ | £ | £ |
| Argentine Republic ... | 6,453,817 | 4,605,942 | 2,838,037 | 911,851 |
| Austria ................ | 26,492,175 | 34,692,487 | 965,809 | 1,204,325 |
| Belgium .................... | ...... | ...... | 2,819,753. | 7,555,207 |
| Brazil .................... | 15,535,795 | 17,664,354 | 5,700,584 | 5,894,069 |
| Chili .................... | 4,171,293 | 5,817,978 | 2,536,801 | 4,417,568 |
| China .................... | 47,700,904 | 34,721,817 | 5,005,190 | 9,340,395 |
| Denmark .................. | ...... | ...... | 1,284,755 | 2,588,921 |
| Egypt .................... | ...... | ...... | 8,189,647 | 15,498,292 |
| Finland .................. | ...... | ...... | 139,950 | 335,603 |
| France .................... | 126,227,560 | 118,892,240 | 12,131,581 | 33,740,660 |
| Gt. Britain & Ireland... | 275,249,853 | 226,057,136 | ...... | ...... |
| Greece .................... | 2,210,706 | 1,121,023 | 956,499 | 1,246,683 |
| Hamburg and Hanse Towns ................ | 58,431,600 | about same as Imports. | 17,246,847 | 9,424,988 |
| Italy ..................... | 40,954,562 | 24,525,471 | 4,865,931 | 3,106,699 |
| Japan .................... | ...... | ...... | 1,546,136 | 317,853 |
| Mecklenburg Schwerin | ...... | ...... | 51,252 | 324,564 |
| Mexico .................. | ...... | ...... | 806,162 | 315,168 |
| Netherlands ............ | 40,000,000 | 32,000,000 | 9,396,567 | 10,823,585 |
| Oldenburg ............... | ...... | ...... | 33,199 | 34,656 |
| Papal States ............ | ...... | ...... | 15,313 | 5,162 |
| Persia .................... | 2,500,000 | 1,500,000 | 14,066 | ...... |
| Peru .................... | 5,000,000 | 6,000,000 | 1,426,448 | 3,701,362 |
| Portugal .................. | ...... | ...... | 2,005,726 | 2,324,090 |
| Prussia .................. | ...... | ...... | 2,886,702 | 7,383,619 |
| Russia .................... | 32,503,932 | 35,293,810 | 3,941,185 | 22,286,926 |
| Spain .................... | 20,000,000 | 12,000,000 | 2,563,219 | 6,088,389 |
| Sweden .................. | 5,831,277 | 6,004,777 | 1,497,550 | 6,477,865 |
| Turkey .................. | ...... | ...... | 7,105,951 | 4,086,475 |
| United States ............ | 91,174,784 | 73,282,098 | 21,821,786 | 41,047,949 |
| Uruguay .................. | ...... | ...... | 1,445,210 | 1,222,228 |

# THE COLONIAL EMPIRE OF GREAT BRITAIN.

*(From Martin's " Statesman's Year-Book.")*

| Colonies and Dependencies. | Date and Mode of Acquisition. | |
|---|---|---|
| **EUROPE.** | | |
| Gibraltar ... ... ... | Capture ... ... | 1704 |
| Heligoland ... ... ... | Cession ... ... | 1814 |
| Malta and Gozo ... ... | Capture ... ... | 1800 |
| **ASIA.** | | |
| Ceylon ... ... ... | Capitulation ... ... | 1796 |
| Bengal ... ... ... | | |
| Bombay ... ... ... | Settlement and Conquest, at | |
| Madras ... ... ... | various periods, fr. 1825 to | 1849 |
| N. W. Provinces ... ... | | |
| Punjaub ... ... ... | | |
| Hong-Kong ... ... ... | Treaty ... ... | 1843 |
| Labuan ... ... ... | Cession ... ... | 1846 |
| **AFRICA.** | | |
| Cape of Good Hope ... ... | Capitulation ... ... | 1806 |
| Gambia ... ... ... | Settlement ... ... | 1631 |
| Gold Coast ... ... ... | Settlement ... ... | 1661 |
| Natal ... ... ... | Settlement ... ... | 1838 |
| St. Helena ... ... ... | Settlement ... ... | 1651 |
| Sierra Leone ... ... ... | Settlement ... ... | 1787 |
| Mauritius ... ... ... | Capitulation ... ... | 1810 |
| **AMERICA.** | | |
| Bermuda ... ... ... | Settlement ... ... | 1609 |
| British Columbia ... ... | Settlement ... ... | — |
| Canada, Lower ... ... | Capitulation and Cession | 1759 |
| Canada, Upper ... ... | | 1763 |
| New Brunswick ... ... | | |
| Newfoundland ... ... | Settlement ... ... | 1497 |
| Nova Scotia ... ... ... | | |
| Prince Edward Island ... ... | | |
| Guiana, British ... ... | Capitulation ... ... | 1803 |
| Falkland Islands ... ... | Cession ... ... | 1837 |
| **WEST INDIES.** | | |
| Antigua and Montserrat ... | Settlement ... ... | 1632 |
| Bahamas ... ... ... | Settlement ... ... | 1629 |
| Barbadoes ... ... ... | Settlement ... ... | 1605 |
| Dominica and Grenada ... | Cession ... ... | 1763 |
| Honduras ... ... ... | Cession ... ... | 1670 |
| Jamaica ... ... ... | Capitulation ... ... | 1655 |
| Nevis ... ... ... | Settlement ... ... | 1628 |
| St. Kitts ... ... ... | Settlement ... | 1624–1650 |
| St. Lucia ... ... ... | Capitulation ... ... | 1803 |
| St. Vincent and Tobago ... | Cession ... ... | 1763 |
| Tortola, &c. ... ... ... | Settlement ... ... | 1665 |
| Trinidad ... ... ... | Capitulation ... ... | 1797 |
| Turk's Island ... ... ... | Settlement ... ... | 1629 |
| **AUSTRALASIA.** | | |
| Australia (South) and Victoria ... | Settlement ... ... | 1836 |
| Australia (West) ... ... | Settlement ... ... | 1829 |
| New South Wales ... ... | Settlement ... ... | 1787 |
| New Zealand ... ... ... | Settlement ... ... | 1839 |
| Queensland ... ... ... | Settlement ... ... | 1859 |
| Tasmania ... ... ... | Settlement ... ... | 1803 |

# IMPORTS AND EXPORTS.

## UNITED KINGDOM, WITH BRITISH POSSESSIONS, FOR 1867.

*(From Martin's " Statesman's Year-Book.")*

|  | IMPORTS. | EXPORTS. |
|---|---|---|
|  | £ | £ |
| Australasia | 12,890,260 | 9,637,157 |
| British Honduras | 180,610 | 148,076 |
| British North America | 6,807,284 | 5,853,523 |
| British West Indies | 5,877,424 | 1,665,054 |
| Cape of Good Hope and Natal | 2,741,285 | 1,893,592 |
| Ceylon | 3,224,512 | 774,754 |
| Channel Islands | 404,083 | 471,284 |
| Gibraltar | 67,720 | 729,231 |
| Hongkong | 183,373 | 2,486,017 |
| India | 25,489,344 | 21,844,619 |
| Malta | 84,471 | 498,909 |
| Mauritius | 889,812 | 376,871 |
| Singapore and Straits | 1,435,839 | 2,068,640 |
| Western Africa | 398,051 | 631,188 |
| Other Possessions | 108,066 | *801,286 |
| Total from British Possessions | £60,783,134 |  |
| Total to British Possessions | | £49,880,201 |

\* Including British Guiana.

## EMIGRATION FROM THE UNITED KINGDOM.

| YEAR. | To the North American Colonies. | To the United States. | To the Australian Colonies and New Zealand. | To Other Places. | TOTAL. |
|---|---|---|---|---|---|
| 1853 | 34,522 | 230,885 | 61,401 | 3,129 | 329,937 |
| 1854 | 43,761 | 193,065 | 83,237 | 3,366 | 323,429 |
| 1855 | 17,966 | 103,414 | 52,309 | 3,118 | 176,807 |
| 1856 | 16,378 | 111,837 | 44,584 | 3,755 | 176,554 |
| 1857 | 21,001 | 126,905 | 61,248 | 3,721 | 212,875 |
| 1858 | 9,704 | 59,716 | 39,295 | 5,257 | 113,972 |
| 1859 | 6,689 | 70,303 | 31,013 | 12,427 | 120,432 |
| 1860 | 9,786 | 87,500 | 24,302 | 6,881 | 128,469 |
| 1861 | 12,707 | 49,764 | 23,738 | 5,561 | 91,770 |
| 1862 | 15,522 | 58,706 | 41,843 | 5,143 | 121,214 |
| 1863 | 18,083 | 146,813 | 53,054 | 5,808 | 223,758 |
| 1864 | 12,721 | 147,042 | 40,942 | 8,195 | 208,900 |
| 1865 | 17,211 | 147,258 | 37,283 | 8,049 | 209,801 |
| 1866 | 13,255 | 161,000 | 24,097 | 6,530 | 204,882 |
| 1867 | 15,503 | 159,275 | 14,466 | 6,709 | 195,953 |

# INTERNATIONAL, INDUSTRIAL, AND FINE ARTS EXHIBITIONS, &c.

*(Compiled for Bradshaw's Diary.)*

| EXHIBITIONS. | OPENED. |
|---|---|
| Great International Exhibition in Hyde Park | 1st May, 1851. |
| Prussian Industrial Exhibition at Berlin | 28th May, 1852. |
| Irish National Exhibition at Cork | 10th June, 1852. |
| Dublin Exhibition | 12th May, 1853. |
| New York Crystal Palace | 14th July, 1853. |
| Victoria (Australian) International Exhibition | 25th October, 1853. |
| Paris Industrial Exhibition | 15th May, 1855. |
| Manchester Art Treasures Exhibition | 5th May, 1857. |
| Antwerp Fine Arts Exhibition | August, 1861. |
| Italian Exhibition at Florence | 14th September, 1861. |
| London International Exhibition | 1st May, 1862. |
| Calcutta Agricultural Exhibition | May, 1863. |
| Amsterdam Industrial Exhibition | August, 1864. |
| Dublin International Exhibition | 9th May, 1865. |
| Cologne Industrial Exhibition | 2nd June, 1865. |
| Moscow Industrial Exhibition | July, 1865. |
| Bristol Industrial Exhibition | 19th September, 1865. |
| Glasgow Industrial Exhibition | 12th December, 1865. |
| Industrial Exhibitions in Metropolitan Districts | 1865 and 1866. |
| York Fine Arts Exhibition | 24th July, 1866. |
| City Industrial Exhibition at Guildhall | 6th March, 1866. |
| Paris International Exhibition | 1st April, 1867. |
| Havre International Exhibition | 1st June, 1868. |
| Leeds Art Treasures | May, 1868. |
| Netherlands International Exhibition | 15th July, 1869. |

# ROYAL AGRICULTURAL SOCIETY'S EXHIBITIONS.

| PLACE. | DATE. | No. of Visitors. | PLACE. | DATE. | No. of Visitors. |
|---|---|---|---|---|---|
| Lewes | 1852 | No accnt. | Canterbury | 1860 | 42,304 |
| Gloucester | 1853 | 36,245 | Leeds | 1861 | 145,738 |
| Lincoln | 1854 | 37,635 | Battersea | 1862 | 124,328 |
| Carlisle | 1855 | No accnt. | Worcester | 1863 | 75,807 |
| Chelmsford | 1856 | 32,982 | Newcastle | 1864 | 114,281 |
| Salisbury | 1857 | 37,342 | Plymouth | 1865 | 88,036 |
| Chester | 1858 | 62,539 | Bury | 1867 | 60,635 |
| Warwick | 1859 | 55,577 | Leicester | 1868 | 96,129 |

# REVENUE AND EXPENDITURE OF THE PRINCIPAL COUNTRIES OF THE WORLD.

*(Compiled and Arranged for Bradshaw's Diary from " Martin's Statesman's Year Book.")*

| COUNTRY. | YEAR. | REVENUE. | | EXPENDITURE. | |
|---|---|---|---|---|---|
| | | Amount of Revenue, Actual or Estimated. | Per head of Population. | Amount of Expenditure, Actual or Estimated. | Per head of Population. |
| | | £ | £ s. d. | £ | £ s. d. |
| Argentine Republic.. | 1867 | 2,497,981 | 1 14 8 | 2,841,155 | 1 17 2 |
| Austria ... ... ... | 1868 | 32,023,052 | 0 19 1 | 37,223,355 | 1 4 10 |
| Baden ... ... ... | 1866 | 1,424,542 | 0 19 11 | 1,624,577 | 1 2 8 |
| Bavaria ... ... ... | 1866-7 | 3,893,383 | 0 16 2 | 3,893,383 | 0 16 2 |
| Belgium ... ... ... | 1866 | 6,561,732 | 1 6 4 | 6,343,170 | 1 5 6 |
| Brazil ... ... ... | 1865-6 | 6,512,539 | 0 13 1 | 13,301,541 | 1 6 3 |
| Brunswick ... ... | 1865-6 | 766,200 | 0 17 5 | 766,200 | 0 17 5 |
| Chili ... ... ... | 1864 | 1,854,984 | 1 2 2 | 1,614,073 | 1 0 8 |
| Denmark ... ... | 1866-7 | 2,974,949 | 1 15 9 | 2,979,237 | 1 15 10 |
| France ... ... ... | 1866 | 74,068,274 | 1 19 1 | 76,358,921 | 2 0 3 |
| Gt. Britain & Ireland | 1867-8 | 69,600,218 | 2 6 3 | 71,766,242 | 2 7 10 |
| Greece ... ... ... | 1865 | 1,005,488 | 0 18 4 | 1,064,994 | 0 19 5 |
| Hungary ... ... | 1868 | 9,968,000 | 0 14 1 | 10,056,700 | 0 14 4 |
| Italy ... ... ... | 1866 | 31,763,766 | 1 8 3 | 36,444,652 | 1 12 5 |
| Netherlands ... ... | 1866 | 9,653,107 | 2 11 8 | 8,823,644 | 2 8 2 |
| Norway ... ... ... | 1865-6 | 1,073,250 | 0 12 7 | 1,073,250 | 0 12 7 |
| Oldenburg ... ... | 1866 | 332,965 | 1 2 1 | 323,565 | 1 1 10 |
| Peru ... ... ... | 1866 | 2,567,295 | 0 18 7 | 2,435,062 | 0 18 5 |
| Portugal ... ... ... | 1866-7 | 3,596,659 | 0 16 4 | 4,748,964 | 1 1 10 |
| Prussia ... ... ... | 1867 | 25,339,480 | 1 1 6 | 25,339,480 | 1 1 6 |
| Russia ... ... ... | 1867 | 70,276,277 | 0 18 11 | 70,276,277 | 0 18 11 |
| Saxony ... ... ... | 1865-6 | 1,663,740 | 0 14 3 | 2,048,847 | 0 17 6 |
| Spain ... ... ... | 1865-6 | 27,493,602 | 1 14 4 | 27,473,323 | 1 14 3 |
| Sweden ... ... ... | 1855-6 | 1,869,298 | 0 9 1 | 2,251,677 | 0 10 11 |
| Switzerland ... ... | 1866 | 767,000 | 0 6 1 | 776,600 | 0 6 2 |
| Turkey ... ... ... | 1864-5 | 14,589,855 | 0 8 3 | 14,425,525 | 0 8 2 |
| United States ... | 1866-7 | 98,126,922 | 2 16 1 | 218,615,931 | 6 6 3 |
| Wurtemburg ... ... | 1866-7 | 4,268,899 | 0 16 3 | 4,268,059 | 0 16 2 |

# BRITISH TARIFF.

## LIST OF CUSTOMS OR IMPORT DUTIES.

| | RATES OF DUTY. | | | | RATES OF DUTY. | | |
|---|---|---|---|---|---|---|---|
| | £ | s. | d. | | £ | s. | d. |
| BEER AND ALE,—all kinds of...*Brl.* | 1 | 0 | 0 | SUGAR :— | | | |
| CARDS, playing......*The Doz. Packs.* | 0 | 3 | 9 | Candy, brown or white, and refined or equal in quality thereto ...... } *Cwt.* | 0 | 12 | 10 |
| CHICORY, or other substitutes for Chicory or Coffee:— | | | | White clayed or equal in quality thereto, not being refined or equal in quality thereto ...... } " | 0 | 11 | 8 |
| Raw or kiln-dried............*Cwt.* | 1 | 6 | 6 | | | | |
| Roasted or ground ......... *Lb.* | 0 | 0 | 4 | | | | |
| CHLOROFORM ........................ " | 0 | 3 | 0 | Yellow Muscovado and brown clayed or equal in quality thetro, & not equal to white clayed } " | 0 | 10 | 0 |
| COCOA, Raw ........................ " | 0 | 0 | 1 | | | | |
| Paste or Chocolate............ " | 0 | 0 | 1 | | | | |
| Husks and Shells............*Cwt.* | 0 | 2 | 0 | Brown Muscovado or equal in quality thereto, and not equal to yellow Muscovado or brown clayed ............. } " | 0 | 9 | 4 |
| COFFEE ........................ *Lb.* | 0 | 0 | 3 | | | | |
| Kiln dried, roasted, or ground ........................ " | 0 | 0 | 4 | | | | |
| CONFECTIONERY, Succades, and dried Cherries ......... } " | 0 | 0 | 1 | Any other Sugar not equal in quality to brown Muscovado...... } " | 0 | 8 | 2 |
| CORN and GRAIN of all kinds...*Cwt.* | 0 | 0 | 3 | CANE JUICE ........................ " | 0 | 0 | 2 |
| MEAL & FLOUR of all kinds, Biscuit, Bread, and Starch } " | 0 | 0 | 4½ | MOLASSES ........................ " | 0 | 3 | 6 |
| COLLODION ........................*Gal.* | 1 | 4 | 0 | TEA ........................ *Lb.* | 0 | 0 | 6 |
| CURRANTS, Figs, Fig-cake, Prunes, and Raisins ...... } *Cwt.* | 0 | 7 | 0 | TOBACCO, unmanufactured, viz : | | | |
| DICE ........................*The Pair.* | 1 | 1 | 0 | Stemmed, stripped, or unstemmed, containing 10 lbs. or more of moisture in every 100 lbs. weight thereof...... } " | 0 | 3 | 0 with 5 per cent. thereon, |
| ESSENCE OF SPRUCE ................. | 10 ⅌ cent. ad val. | | | | | | |
| *ETHER, Sulphuric .................*Gal.* | 1 | 5 | 0 | | | | |
| MALT........................*The Quarter.* | 1 | 5 | 0 | ——— containing less than 10 lbs. of moisture in every 100 lbs. weight thereof...... } " | 0 | 3 | 6 |
| PICKLES, preserved in Vinegar..*Gal.* | 0 | 0 | 1 | | | | |
| PLATE, Gold ........................*Oz. Troy.* | 0 | 17 | 0 | | | | |
| Silver, gilt or ungilt ...... " | 0 | 1 | 6 | TOBACCO, manufactured, viz.: | | | |
| PLUMS, dried or preserved (except in Sugar)............. } *Cwt.* | 0 | 7 | 0 | Cigars ........................ " | 0 | 5 | 0 |
| | | | | Cavendish or Negrohead... " | 0 | 4 | 6 |
| Preserved in Sugar ...... *Lb.* | 0 | 0 | 1 | Snuff, containing more than 13 lbs. of moisture in every 100 lbs. weight thereof ...................... } " | 0 | 3 | 9 |
| POWDER, Hair & other kinds...*Cwt.* | 0 | 0 | 4½ | | | | |
| SPIRITS AND STRONG WATERS, unsweetened :— | | | | | | | |
| Brandy and Geneva..*Proof Gal.* | 0 | 10 | 5 | ——— not containing more than 13 lbs. of moisture in every 100 lbs. weight thereof...................... } " | 0 | 4 | 6 |
| Rum, of and from any Foreign country, being the country of its production ...... } " | 0 | 10 | 2 | | | | |
| | | | | Other manufactured Tobacco........................ } " | 0 | 4 | 0 |
| Rum from any country, not being the country of its production ...... } " | 0 | 10 | 5 | | | | |
| | | | | Cavendish or Negrohead tobacco, manufactured in bond in the United Kingdom from unmanufactured Tobacco on the entry thereof for home consumption ... } " | 0 | 4 | 0 |
| Tafia of and from any colony of France, and Rum and Spirits of and from a British Possession ............... } " | 0 | 10 | 2 | | | | |
| | | | | | | | |
| Unenumerated ................. " | 0 | 10 | 5 | VARNISH, viz.:— | | | |
| OTHER SPIRITS, sweetened or mixed so that the degree of strength cannot be ascertained by Sykes' Hydrometer : | | | | Containing any quantity of alcohol or spirit ... } *Gal.* | 0 | 12 | 0 |
| | | | | VINEGAR ........................ " | 0 | 0 | 3 |
| | | | | WINE, and Lees of Wine:— | | | |
| Rum, Shrub, Liqueurs, and Cordials of & from a British Possession... } *Gal.* | 0 | 10 | 2 | Under 26 degrees of Proof Spirit............. } " | 0 | 1 | 0 |
| | | | | Under 42° and in bottles | 0 | 2 | 6 |
| Perfumed Spirits, for Perfumery only, and Water, Cologne, not in flasks ................. } " | 0 | 14 | 0 | and an additional Duty of 3d. per Gallon for every degree of strength beyond the highest above specified. | | | |
| Water, Cologne, in flasks (not more than thirty flasks to the Gallon)... } *Per flask* | 0 | 0 | 6 | | | | |
| Unenumerated ............. *Gal.* | 0 | 14 | 0 | | | | |

NOTE.—No Export Duties are levied in the United Kingdom.
* The various sorts of Spirituous Ether are charged according to the amount of Proof Spirit they contain.

# TABLE OF LATITUDE, AND DIFFERENCE OF TIME OR LONGITUDE, OF PLACES IN THE WORLD.

[The Longitudes are reckoned from the Meridian of Greenwich.]

(*Compiled for Bradshaw's Diary.*)

| PLACES. | LATITUDE of PLACES | | East of Greenwich, or *before* Greenwich Time. | | West of Greenwich, or *after* Greenwich Time. | | |
|---|---|---|---|---|---|---|---|
| | | | Hrs. | Mins. | Hrs. | Mins. | |
| Alexandria | 31° 13' | N | 2 | 0 | ... | ... | E |
| Altona | 53° 33' | N | ... | 40 | ... | ... | E |
| Athens | 37° 58' | N | 1 | 35 | ... | ... | E |
| Berlin | 52° 30' | N | ... | 54 | ... | ... | E |
| Bologna | 44° 30' | N | ... | 45 | ... | ... | E |
| Bombay | 18° 56' | N | 4 | 52 | ... | ... | E |
| Bonn | 50° 44' | N | ... | 28 | ... | ... | E |
| Breslau | 51° 7' | N | 1 | 8 | ... | ... | E |
| Brussels | 50° 51' | N | ... | 17 | ... | ... | E |
| Cadiz | 36° 28' | N | ... | ... | ... | 25 | W |
| Calcutta | 22° 34' | N | 5 | 53 | ... | ... | E |
| Cambridge (U.S.) | 42° 23' | N | ... | ... | 4 | 45 | W |
| Canton | 23° 7' | N | 7 | 33 | ... | ... | E |
| Constantinople | 41° 1' | S | 1 | 56 | ... | ... | E |
| Cape of Good Hope | 33° 56' | N | 1 | 14 | ... | ... | E |
| Christiania | 59° 55' | N | ... | 43 | ... | ... | E |
| Copenhagen | 55° 41' | N | ... | 50 | ... | ... | E |
| Florence | 43° 46' | N | ... | 45 | ... | ... | E |
| Geneva | 46° 12' | N | ... | 25 | ... | ... | E |
| Gibraltar | 36° 6' | N | ... | ... | ... | 21 | W |
| Gottingen | 51° 32' | N | ... | 40 | ... | ... | E |
| Gotha | 50° 56' | N | ... | 43 | ... | ... | E |
| Greenwich | 51° 29' | N | ... | ... | ... | ... | ... |
| Hamburgh | 53° 33' | N | ... | 40 | ... | ... | E |
| Konisberg | 54° 43' | N | 1 | 22 | ... | ... | E |
| Leipsic | 51° 20' | N | ... | 50 | ... | ... | E |
| Lisbon | 38° 42' | N | ... | ... | ... | 37 | W |
| Madras | 13° 4' | N | 5 | 21 | ... | ... | E |
| Marseilles | 43° 18' | N | ... | 21 | ... | ... | E |
| Melbourne | 37° 50' | S | 9 | 40 | ... | ... | E |
| Milan | 45° 28' | N | ... | 37 | ... | ... | E |
| Moscow | 55° 45' | N | 2 | 30 | ... | ... | E |
| Munich | 48° 9' | N | ... | 46 | ... | ... | E |
| Naples | 40° 52' | N | ... | 57 | ... | ... | E |
| New York | 40° 43' | N | ... | ... | 5 | 15 | W |
| Palermo | 38° 6' | N | ... | 53 | ... | ... | E |
| Paris | 48° 50' | N | ... | 9 | ... | ... | E |
| Prague | 50° 5' | N | ... | 58 | ... | ... | E |
| St. Petersburgh | 59° 56' | N | 2 | 1 | ... | ... | E |
| Quebec | 46° 49' | N | ... | ... | 4 | 45 | W |
| Rio de Janeiro | 22° 54' | S | ... | ... | 2 | 52 | W |
| Rome | 41° 54' | N | ... | 50 | ... | ... | E |
| San Francisco | 37° 48' | N | ... | ... | 8 | 10 | W |
| Santiago | 33° 26' | S | ... | ... | 4 | 43 | W |
| Stockholm | 59° 21' | N | 1 | 12 | ... | ... | E |
| Sydney | 33° 52' | S | 10 | 5 | ... | ... | E |
| Turin | 45° 4' | N | ... | 31 | ... | ... | E |
| Utrecht | 52° 5' | N | ... | 21 | ... | ... | E |
| Venice | 45° 26' | N | ... | 49 | ... | ... | E |
| Vienna | 48° 13' | N | 1 | 6 | ... | ... | E |
| Warsaw | 52° 13' | N | 1 | 24 | ... | ... | E |
| Washington | 38° 54' | N | ... | ... | 5 | 8 | W |

# ENGLISH SEA-COAST TOWNS.

*(Geographical Table compiled specially for Bradshaw's Diary.)*

| SEA-COAST TOWNS. | In what County. | Latitude N. | | Longitude. | | East or West of Greenwich. | Sea Aspect. | Population per last Census. | Distance from London. |
|---|---|---|---|---|---|---|---|---|---|
| | | ° | ′ | ° | ′ | | | | Miles. |
| Blackpool ... ... | Lancashire ... | 53 | 49 | 3 | 4 | W | W.N.W | 3,506 | 229 |
| Bognor ... ... | Sussex ... | 50 | 47 | 0 | 42 | W | S.S.E | 2,523 | 66 |
| Bournemouth ... | Hampshire ... | 50 | 49 | 1 | 53 | W | S.S.W | 1,940 | 111 |
| Bridlington... ... | Yorkshire ... | 54 | 8 | 0 | 10 | W | S.S.W | 8,452 | 205 |
| Brighton ... ... | Sussex ... | 50 | 50 | 0 | 6 | W | S.S.E | 77,693 | 50 |
| Broadstairs... ... | Kent ... | 51 | 21 | 1 | 27 | E | E.S.E | 2,855 | 77 |
| Cromer ... ... | Norfolk ... | 52 | 55 | 1 | 20 | E | N.N.E | 1,367 | 114 |
| Dawlish ... ... | Devonshire ... | 50 | 36 | 3 | 26 | W | S.E | 3,505 | 206 |
| Deal and Walmer. | Kent ... | 51 | 13 | 1 | 24 | E | E.S.E | 10,806 | 90 |
| Dover ... ... ... | Kent ... | 51 | 8 | 1 | 19 | E | S.S.E | 25,325 | 76 |
| Eastbourne... ... | Sussex ... | 50 | 46 | 0 | 17 | E | S.S.E | 5,795 | 66 |
| Exmouth ... ... | Devonshire ... | 50 | 29 | 3 | 25 | W | S.S.W | 5,228 | 182 |
| Filey ... ... ... | Yorkshire ... | 54 | 15 | 0 | 12 | W | E | 2,244 | 217 |
| Folkestone ... ... | Kent ... | 51 | 5 | 1 | 11 | E | S.S.E | 8,507 | 71 |
| Hastings and St. } Leonards on Sea } | Sussex ...<br>Sussex ... | 50<br>50 | 53<br>53 | 0<br>0 | 35<br>36 | E<br>E | S<br>S } | 24,530 | 62 |
| Herne Bay ... ... | Kent ... | 51 | 23 | 1 | 8 | E | N.N.E | 3,147 | 66 |
| Hythe... ... ... | Kent ... | 51 | 4 | 1 | 5 | E | S.S.E | 3,001 | 68 |
| Ilfracombe ... ... | N. Devonshire... | 51 | 14 | 4 | 5 | W | N.N.E | 3,034 | 211 |
| Llandudno ... ... | North Wales ... | 53 | 17 | 3 | 39 | W | N.N.E | 2,316 | 227 |
| Lowestoft ... ... | Norfolk ... | 52 | 29 | 1 | 44 | E | E.S.E | 10,663 | 117 |
| Margate ... ... | Kent ... | 51 | 23 | 1 | 24 | E | N.N.E | 8,874 | 74 |
| Penzance ... ... | Cornwall... ... | 50 | 7 | 5 | 31 | W | S.S.E | 9,414 | 327 |
| Ramsgate ... ... | Kent ... | 51 | 20 | 1 | 26 | E | E.S.E | 11,865 | 79 |
| Rhyl ... ... ... | North Wales ... | 53 | 19 | 3 | 27 | W | N.N.E | 2,965 | 209 |
| Ryde ... ... ... | Isle of Wight... | 50 | 44 | 1 | 11 | W | E.S.E | 9,269 | 80 |
| Sandgate ... ... | Kent ... | 51 | 5 | 1 | 9 | E | S.S.E | 1,743 | 73 |
| Sandown ... ... | Isle of Wight... | 50 | 40 | 1 | 10 | W | S.E. by E | 3,000 | 89 |
| Scarboro' ... ... | Yorkshire ... | 54 | 24 | 0 | 18 | W | E S.E | 18,377 | 227 |
| Shanklin ... ... | Isle of Wight... | 50 | 39 | 1 | 11 | W | S.E. | 479 | 91 |
| Southend ... ... | Essex ... | 51 | 16 | 0 | 42 | E | S.S.W | 1,500 | 42 |
| Southport ... ... | Lancashire ... | 53 | 39 | 3 | 3 | W | W.N.W | 8,940 | 212 |
| Tenby ... ... ... | Pembroke ... | 51 | 40 | 4 | 41 | W | S.S.E | 2,982 | 269 |
| Torquay ... ... | Devonshire ... | 50 | 28 | 3 | 30 | W | S.S.W | 16,419 | 220 |
| Walton on the Naze | Essex ... | 51 | 52 | 1 | 17 | E | E.S.E | 750 | 70 |
| Weymouth... ... | Dorsetshire ... | 52 | 40 | 2 | 34 | W | S.S.E | 11,383 | 142 |
| Whitby ... ... | Yorkshire ... | 54 | 30 | 0 | 24 | W | E | 12,051 | 248 |
| Worthing ... ... | Sussex ... | 50 | 49 | 0 | 22 | E | S.S.E | 5,805 | 61 |
| Ventnor ... ... | Isle of Wight... | 50 | 37 | 1 | 12 | W | S | 3,208 | 93 |
| Yarmouth ... ... | Norfolk ... ... | 52 | 37 | 1 | 44 | E | E.S.E. | 34,810 | 147 |

# LENGTH OF DAYLIGHT, &c.

*(A Table of Daybreak, Sun Rise and Sun Set, Length of Day, &c., at and near London, compiled for Bradshaw's Diary from "Partridge's Stationers' Almanac.")*

(MEAN, OR CLOCK TIME.)

| Day of Month. | Break of Day. h. m. | Sun Rise. h. m. | Sun Set. h. m. | Length of Day. h. m. | Day of Month. | Break of Day. h. m. | Sun Rise. h. m. | Sun Set. h. m. | Length of Day. h. m. |
|---|---|---|---|---|---|---|---|---|---|
| JAN. 1 | 6 2 | 8 8 | 3 59 | 7 51 | JULY 1 | *No Night Twilight.* | 3 49 | 8 18 | 16 29 |
| 6 | 6 2 | 8 7 | 4 5 | 7 58 | 6 | | 3 53 | 8 16 | 16 23 |
| 11 | 6 1 | 8 5 | 4 12 | 8 7 | 11 | | 3 58 | 8 12 | 16 15 |
| 16 | 5 59 | 8 0 | 4 20 | 8 19 | 16 | | 4 4 | 8 8 | 16 5 |
| 21 | 5 55 | 7 55 | 4 28 | 8 32 | 21 | 0 8 | 4 10 | 8 2 | 15 53 |
| 26 | 5 50 | 7 50 | 4 37 | 8 47 | 26 | 1 1 | 4 17 | 7 56 | 15 39 |
| FEB. 1 | 5 43 | 7 40 | 4 47 | 9 6 | AUG. 1 | 1 32 | 4 26 | 7 46 | 15 21 |
| 6 | 5 36 | 7 32 | 4 57 | 9 24 | 6 | 1 51 | 4 33 | 7 38 | 15 5 |
| 11 | 5 29 | 7 23 | 5 6 | 9 42 | 11 | 2 8 | 4 41 | 7 29 | 14 48 |
| 16 | 5 20 | 7 14 | 5 15 | 10 0 | 16 | 2 24 | 4 49 | 7 19 | 14 31 |
| 21 | 5 11 | 7 4 | 5 24 | 10 19 | 21 | 2 39 | 4 57 | 7 9 | 14 13 |
| 26 | 5 1 | 6 53 | 5 33 | 10 39 | 26 | 2 52 | 5 5 | 6 58 | 13 54 |
| MAR. 1 | 4 54 | 6 47 | 5 38 | 10 51 | SEP. 1 | 3 7 | 5 14 | 6 45 | 13 31 |
| 6 | 4 43 | 6 36 | 5 47 | 11 10 | 6 | 3 19 | 5 22 | 6 34 | 13 12 |
| 11 | 4 31 | 6 25 | 5 56 | 11 30 | 11 | 3 30 | 5 30 | 6 22 | 12 53 |
| 16 | 4 19 | 6 13 | 6 4 | 11 50 | 16 | 3 40 | 5 38 | 6 11 | 12 33 |
| 21 | 4 6 | 6 2 | 6 13 | 12 10 | 21 | 3 50 | 5 46 | 6 0 | 12 14 |
| 26 | 3 53 | 5 50 | 6 21 | 12 30 | 26 | 4 0 | 5 55 | 5 48 | 11 54 |
| APR. 1 | 3 37 | 5 37 | 6 31 | 12 54 | OCT. 1 | 4 9 | 6 3 | 5 36 | 11 34 |
| 6 | 3 23 | 5 25 | 6 39 | 13 13 | 6 | 4 18 | 6 11 | 5 25 | 11 15 |
| 11 | 3 8 | 5 14 | 6 48 | 13 32 | 11 | 4 26 | 6 19 | 5 14 | 10 55 |
| 16 | 2 52 | 5 3 | 6 56 | 13 52 | 16 | 4 35 | 6 28 | 5 3 | 10 36 |
| 21 | 2 36 | 4 53 | 7 4 | 14 11 | 21 | 4 43 | 6 37 | 4 53 | 10 17 |
| 26 | 2 19 | 4 43 | 7 12 | 14 29 | 26 | 4 51 | 6 45 | 4 43 | 9 58 |
| MAY 1 | 2 2 | 4 33 | 7 21 | 14 47 | NOV. 1 | 5 1 | 6 56 | 4 31 | 9 36 |
| 6 | 1 44 | 4 24 | 7 29 | 15 4 | 6 | 5 8 | 7 5 | 4 22 | 9 18 |
| 11 | 1 24 | 4 16 | 7 37 | 15 20 | 11 | 5 16 | 7 14 | 4 15 | 9 1 |
| 16 | 0 59 | 4 8 | 7 44 | 15 35 | 16 | 5 23 | 7 22 | 4 7 | 8 45 |
| 21 | 0 25 | 4 2 | 7 51 | 15 49 | 21 | 5 30 | 7 31 | 4 1 | 8 31 |
| 26 | ... | 3 56 | 7 58 | 16 2 | 26 | 5 36 | 7 39 | 3 56 | 8 18 |
| JUNE 1 | *No Night but all Twilight.* | 3 50 | 8 5 | 16 14 | DEC. 1 | 5 42 | 7 46 | 3 52 | 8 6 |
| 6 | | 3 47 | 8 10 | 16 23 | 6 | 5 48 | 7 53 | 3 50 | 7 57 |
| 11 | | 3 45 | 8 14 | 16 29 | 11 | 5 52 | 7 59 | 3 49 | 7 50 |
| 16 | | 3 44 | 8 17 | 16 33 | 16 | 5 56 | 8 3 | 3 49 | 7 46 |
| 21 | | 3 45 | 8 18 | 16 34 | 21 | 5 59 | 8 6 | 3 51 | 7 44 |
| 26 | | 3 46 | 8 19 | 16 33 | 26 | 6 1 | 8 8 | 3 54 | 7 45 |

# MOONLIGHT.

## MOON'S RISING AND SETTING.

At 4 days old, it sets at, and shines till about 10 at night.
5, do. about 11 „
6, do. about 12 „
7, at or near 1 in the morning.
8, do. 2 do.

At 15, at full, it rises about 6 in the even.
16, at a quarter after 7 „
17, half-past 8 „
18, about 10 „
19, about 11 „
20, about 12 „

NOTE.—This Table is sufficiently accurate for the purpose of ascertaining moonlight evenings.

# TIDES ON THE COAST OF THE UNITED KINGDOM.

The following particulars relating to the Tides along the Coasts of England, Scotland, and the Irish Channel, have been compiled for Bradshaw's Diary, from the Seaman's Almanack, &c.

A CAREFUL investigation of the tides in the Irish Channel, the English Channel, and in the North Sea, has shown the possibility of referring the movements of the several streams to a common standard. For the entrance of the English Channel and North Sea the time of high water at Dover may be considered the standard; and for the whole of the Irish Channel, the time of high water on the shore at the entrance of Liverpool.

Off the mouth of the English Channel the stream will be found running to the *northward and eastward*, while the water is *falling* at Dover; and to the *southward and westward* while it is *rising* at that port. To the southward of the parallel of Scilly, the tides of the Channel and offing blend together with varying force and direction, and occasion the stream to be constantly changing, and in some places even to make the entire circuit of the compass in one tide, without ever remaining long upon any one point. From the parallel of Scilly to the Bristol Channel the stream is more regular, and while the water is *falling* at Dover, will be found setting to the *northward*: near the coast partaking of the direction of the shore, and turning sharply round Trevose Head and Hartland Point into the Bristol Channel; and while the water is *rising* at Dover, setting as sharply out of the Bristol Channel and along the land towards Scilly.

In the North Sea the general features of the streams correspond exactly with those of the English Channel, but the *direction* of the stream is reversed. As soon as the intermediate tide is passed, on coming from the westward, a ship enters the True Stream, which extends from the North Foreland to a line joining the Leman and Ower Light and the Texel. To the northward between the Ower and Texel a mixed tide occurs, similar to that which is experienced off the Start, occasioned by the Channel Stream encountering that of the Offing Stream; and beyond these limits the time of slack water varies with the advance of the tidal hour, as at the entrance of the English Channel; and with this peculiarity also, that in a very short distance there occurs a difference of three hours in the time of slack water.

The tides about Plymouth Sound are tolerably regular, both flood and ebb, generally running each way about six hours and ten minutes at a mean. In Hamoaze the flood stream continues to run up, on spring tides, about fifteen minutes after high water at Devonport Dockyard.

It is high water in Catwater and at the Breakwater rather earlier than at the Dockyard.

In Portland and Weymouth Roads there is very little tide, and it is moderate along the shore from Weymouth to St. Alban's Head.

At the Needles, at full and change, the western stream makes at 10h. 0m., and the flood or eastern stream at at 3h. 40m., and the velocity of both streams over the Bridge and in the South Channel is from 3 to 4 knots; but between Hurst Point and the Island, 5¼ knots, and to the southward of the Bridge about 2 knots. In the Solent the eastern or flood stream makes at 4h., and near the Bramble at 4h. 30m.

At Spithead, at full and change, the eastern stream makes about 2 o'clock, 2¼ hours after high water in the harbour, and runs 7 hours S.E. by S.; and the western stream about 9 o'clock, 2¼ hours before high water in the harbour, and runs 5 hours N.W. by N.

The stream between Beachy and Fairlight continues eastward until 12 o'clock, and westward of Dungeness till half-past 1; 3 leagues from the shore off Dungeness, and, from the S. Foreland, it runs to the E. until 2h. 45m.

About 1 mile S.S.E. of the South Foreland Lighthouse, the stream begins to set to the eastward about 1h. 30m. before high water on the shore at Dover, and runs from N.E. by E. to E.N.E. till 4 hours after high water; it then turns and sets W.S.W. ¼ W. about seven hours. At Dover the flowing stream very seldom continues more than 5 hours, and sometimes scarcely so much; it is nearly the same at Ramsgate. To the northward of the South Foreland the streams change their direction to the N.E. ½ N. and S.W. ½ S.

In the Downs the north-eastern stream begins about 1h. 20m. before high water at Dover, and continues to run 5h. 30m.; it then turns and runs in a contrary direction till 2 hours before the ensuing high water.

In the Gull Stream, 1 mile N.N.W. from the Bunthead, the northern stream begins at 1h. 10m. before high water at Dover, and continues for 6 hours; it then turns and runs in a contrary direction till 1½ hours before the ensuing high water.

In the North Sea the flood tide-wave enters from the Atlantic Ocean between the coast of Norway and the British Isles, and passes through the various channels formed by the Shetlands, the Orkneys, and the north point of Scotland. The average rate of the stream in the offing is very moderate, not exceeding 1½ knots; but that part of the stream which enters by the Pentland Firth acquires a furious rapidity, amounting at spring tides even to 8 knots. Immediately on quitting the Firth it abates in strength, as it diverges into open water; its eastern branch filling up the basin of the North Sea as it advances towards the coast of Jutland and Holland; whilst its western branch, more or less confined by the Dogger and other outlying banks, swells along the shores of Scotland and England, and makes high water in all their rivers and harbours successively till it arrives in the Thames.

At 2 miles without the Bell Rock Lighthouse the flood continues running to the southward till 2h. 55m. after high water at Leith; but between the Bell Rock and Fifeness it changes 2 hours earlier.

At 3 or 4 miles off Hartlepool, and at the same distance off Whitby, the flood stream runs to the southward till 4h. 10m. after high water at Leith; and at the same distance off Flamborough Head it continues to run half an hour longer. Near the Norfolk and Suffolk coasts the streams of tide run nearly parallel to the shore. Off Wells the flood runs to the eastward till 9 o'clock or three hours after high water on the shore.

Four miles off Cromer, and the same distance off Hasborough, the flood stream runs along the shore to the southward till 10h. 15m., or 1h. 45m. before high water at Harwich, and the ebb in a contrary direction.

At 2½ miles off Lowestoft the flood stream continues to run to the S.S.W. till 1h. 30m. before high water at Harwich.

At Margate it is high water about 11h. 40m. by the ground. Near the East buoy of Margate Sand, at the first of the flood, on the shore the stream sets S. by W., veering westward, till about half flood, or 9h. 15m., it sets west, and continues veering, till at high water it falls slack at N.N.W. The ebb stream begins at N.E., veering eastward, and increasing in strength till about half ebb, or 2h. 45m., when it sets S.E. by E., still veering, and the latter part with diminished velocity, till at low water it falls slack at south.

The direction of strong winds, and the varying pressure of the atmosphere, considerably affect both the times and the heights of high water. In the North Sea a strong N.N.W. gale and a low barometer raise the surface 2 or 3 feet higher, and cause the tide to flow from the Pentland Firth to London half an hour longer than the times given in the Tables. Easterly, S.E., and S.W. winds produce opposite effects, which will be felt as far down the channel as Dungeness. On the contrary, at the entrance of the Channel, and as far as Portland, south-westerly winds, with a low barometer, raise the surface of the water; and north-easterly winds and a high barometer lower it.

# HIGH WATER TABLE.

The following List, showing the difference of Time, between London and the Outports of the United Kingdom, as well as some of the Foreign Ports, is taken from Local Tide Tables and the best books on Navigation.

*(Compiled for Bradshaw's Diary.)*

| | h. m. | | | h. m. |
|---|---|---|---|---|
| Aberdeen | sub. 0 55 | Heligoland | — | 2 34 |
| Alderney Pier | add 4 39 | Hellevoetsluys | add | 0 9 |
| Antwerp | — 2 18 | Holyhead Harbour | sub. | 3 42 |
| Ardrishaig | sub. 2 14 | Horne Point | — | 0 22 |
| Ayr Harbour | — 1 57 | Hull | add | 4 22 |
| Bantry Bay (Castletown) | add 2 7 | Hythe | sub. | 3 21 |
| Barnstaple Bar | — 3 23 | Ilfracombe | add | 3 35 |
| Beachy Head | sub. 2 47 | Jersey (St. Aubyn) | — | 4 14 |
| Beaumaris | — 3 41 | Kingstown Harbour | sub. | 2 57 |
| Belfast | — 3 24 | Kinsale Harbour | add | 2 36 |
| Berwick | add 0 12 | Leith | — | 0 10 |
| Blakeney Harbour | — 4 23 | Lerwick Harbour | sub. | 4 22 |
| Boulogne | sub. 2 40 | Little Hampton | — | 2 21 |
| Brest Harbour | add 1 40 | Liverpool | — | 2 44 |
| Brighton | sub. 2 45 | Lough Foyle (Londonderry) | add | 5 52 |
| Bristol | add 5 10 | Margate | sub. | 1 55 |
| Calais | sub. 2 18 | Milford Haven, entrance to | add | 3 39 |
| Campbelton | — 2 22 | Montrose | sub. | 0 42 |
| Cape Clear | add 1 54 | Morlaix Road | add | 2 46 |
| Cardigan Bar | — 4 30 | Mount's Bay | — | 2 23 |
| Carmarthen Bay | — 3 52 | Newhaven | sub. | 2 15 |
| Chatham | sub. 1 13 | Newport (Isle of Wight) | — | 3 13 |
| Cherbourg | add 5 42 | New Shoreham Harbour | — | 2 37 |
| Chichester Harbour | sub. 2 37 | Nore Light | — | 0 58 |
| Christchurch Harbour | — 5 7 | Ostend | — | 1 40 |
| Cork Harbour (Queenstown) | add 2 54 | Peel Harbour, Isle of Man | — | 2 59 |
| Cowes, West | sub. 3 21 | Pembroke Dock-Yard | add | 4 55 |
| Crinan | add 2 42 | Penzance | — | 2 23 |
| Cromarty | sub. 2 11 | Plymouth | — | 3 26 |
| Cuxhaven | — 1 23 | Port Glasgow | sub. | 2 49 |
| Dartmouth Harbour | add 4 3 | Port Patrick | — | 2 57 |
| Devonport Dock-Yard | — 3 36 | Portsmouth Harbour | — | 2 27 |
| Dieppe | sub. 3 1 | Ramsey Harbour, Isle of Man | — | 2 55 |
| Donegal Bar | add 2 53 | Ramsgate Harbour | — | 2 26 |
| Douglas Harbour, Isle of Man | sub. 2 56 | Rye Bay | — | 2 47 |
| Dover Harbour | — 2 56 | Scarborough | add | 2 4 |
| Dublin | — 2 54 | Scilly Islands | — | 2 35 |
| Dundee | add 0 24 | Shannon Mouth | — | 2 23 |
| Dunkirk | sub. 1 59 | Sligo Bay | — | 3 11 |
| Exmouth Bar | add 4 13 | Southampton | sub. | 3 37 |
| Eyemouth | add 0 8 | Southend and Sheerness | — | 1 27 |
| Falmouth Harbour | — 3 23 | Spurn Point, the | add | 3 19 |
| Flushing (Walcheren) | sub. 0 47 | St. Ives | — | 2 37 |
| Folkestone | — 3 21 | St. Malo | — | 3 48 |
| Fort George | — 2 6 | Stromness | sub. | 5 7 |
| Galway | add 2 23 | Sunderland | add | 1 15 |
| Glenluce Bay | sub. 3 26 | Texel Road | add | 5 16 |
| Gravelines | — 2 26 | Torbay | — | 3 54 |
| Gravesend | — 0 37 | Tynemouth Bar | — | 1 13 |
| Greenock | — 1 59 | Waterford | — | 3 43 |
| Guernsey Pier | add 4 24 | Wells Harbour | — | 3 54 |
| Hamburg | — 3 25 | West Scheldt, entrance | sub. | 1 31 |
| Hartlepool | — 1 21 | Weymouth | add | 4 23 |
| Harwich | sub. 2 37 | Whitby | — | 1 38 |
| Hastings | — 3 14 | Wigton Bay | sub. | 3 7 |
| Havre | — 4 14 | Yarmouth Roads | — | 4 52 |

EXPLANATION:—To find the time of High Water at the above places, it will be necessary to add or subtract the numbers in the above Table, according to the directions here given, to or from the time of High Water at London. The time of High Water at London Bridge is given in most of the London daily newspapers.

For example:—On the 2nd of January, the morning High Water at London Bridge is 4h. 32m.; the High Water at Dover Harbour is 2h. 56m. earlier; subtract, according to the direction, 2h. 56m. from 4h. 32m., and the time of High Water at Dover Harbour on that day will be found to be at 1h. 36m. in the morning.

# MEAN TEMPERATURE AT PLACES IN VARIOUS PARTS OF THE WORLD.

*(Compiled for Bradshaw's Diary.)*

| PLACE. | COUNTRY. | MONTHS.* | | | | | | | | | | | |
|---|---|---|---|---|---|---|---|---|---|---|---|---|---|
| | | Jan | Feb | Mr. | Apl | My | Jne | Jly. | Ag. | Spt | Oct | No. | Dec |
| Berlin ... | Prussia ... | 28 | 32 | 38 | 47 | 56 | 63 | 66 | 65 | 58 | 50 | 39 | 35 |
| Cairo ... | Egypt ... | 58 | 56 | 64 | 77 | 78 | 84 | 86 | 86 | 79 | 72 | 63 | 61 |
| England ... | Vsia ... | 36 | 39 | 42 | 47 | 56 | 59 | 63 | 63 | 58 | 51 | 43 | 39 |
| Jerusalem | — | 48 | 54 | 60 | 54 | 67 | 72 | 74 | 72 | 72 | 68 | 59 | 47 |
| Lisbon ... | Portugal | 53 | 53 | 56 | 59 | 64 | 69 | 73 | 71 | 69 | 63 | 56 | 52 |
| Madrid ... | Spain ... | 43 | 45 | 48 | 55 | 63 | 72 | 78 | 79 | 68 | 56 | 48 | 43 |
| Messina ... | Sicily ... | 54 | 54 | 57 | 61 | 67 | 74 | 78 | 79 | 76 | 69 | 63 | 57 |
| New Zealand | Australasia | 65 | 67 | 65 | 61 | 55 | 53 | 51 | 53 | 54 | 59 | 61 | 67 |
| Paris ... | France ... | 36 | 40 | 44 | 50 | 58 | 63 | 66 | 65 | 60 | 52 | 44 | 39 |
| Philadelphia | U. States | 30 | 29 | 39 | 49 | 61 | 69 | 74 | 72 | 63 | 51 | 40 | 31 |
| Sebastopol | Crimea ... | 34 | 37 | 42 | 51 | 62 | 70 | 71 | 70 | 64 | 54 | 44 | 37 |
| Toronto ... | Canada ... | 25 | 24 | 30 | 43 | 53 | 61 | 66 | 67 | 59 | 46 | 36 | 27 |
| Turin ... | Italy ... | 30 | 36 | 44 | 53 | 64 | 69 | 73 | 73 | 64 | 54 | 43 | 33 |
| Petersburg | Russia ... | 15 | 19 | 25 | 37 | 48 | 60 | 64 | 61 | 51 | 41 | 30 | 23 |
| Vienna ... | Austria ... | 29 | 34 | 40 | 52 | 62 | 67 | 70 | 70 | 70 | 51 | 40 | 33 |

\* The figures under each Month denote the mean degree of temperature at each place.

## POINTS OF THE COMPASS FROM WHICH THE WINDS BLOW IN ENGLAND.

The following shows the comparative Points of the Compass from which the winds blow in England, as ascertained from averages taken by Mr. Glaisher of the Royal Observatory :—

| | | | | | | | |
|---|---|---|---|---|---|---|---|
| From the South West | ...... | 104 days. | From the East | ...... | ...... | 22 days. |
| ,, North East | ...... | 48 ,, | ,, South East | ...... | 20 ,, |
| ,, North | ...... | 41 ,, | Calm | ...... | ...... | ...... | 34 ,, |
| ,, West | ...... | 38 ,, | | |
| ,, South | ...... | 34 ,, | | 365 days. |
| ,, North West | ...... | 24 ,, | | |

It will be seen that the prevailing winds in England are from the South West and North East; that the South West is the predominant wind for eight months of the year, and the North East prevails from one to two months.

## CLIMATE OF INDIA.

*January.*—Thermometer ranges from 52° to 65° in the shade.

*February.*—Thermometer 58° to 75°, beginning of the month generally cool and comfortable to Europeans, but frequently disagreeable and unhealthy about middle.

*March.*—Thermometer 68° to 82°.

*April.*—Thermometer 80° to 90°.

*May.*—Thermometer 85° to 98°. The most trying month of the year, the heat most oppressive, and at times most unbearable.

*June.*—Thermometer frequently rises to 99°, the weather exceedingly oppressive to the last degree, and many deaths arise from sunstroke; but the periodical rains usually set in about the 15th, and the air becomes cooler.

*July.*—Thermometer 80° to 90°, but there is generally much rain, and the weather then becomes cool and agreeable.

*August.*—Thermometer 80° to 90°. Rainy weather, with gales of wind.

*September.*—Thermometer 75° to 80°. Rain subsides, but winds continue.

*October.*—Thermometer 74° to 85°. Frequent rain till about 20th.

*November.*—Thermometer 68° to 75°. Pleasant weather; morning and evenings cool.

*December.*—Thermometer 58° to 60°. To Europeans, this and the preceding are the pleasantest months in the year; the weather is generally cool and fine.

# TABLE OF DISTANCES BETWEEN CERTAIN SEA-PORTS IN THE UNITED KINGDOM AND ABROAD.

*(Compiled for Bradshaw's Diary.)*

| SEAPORTS. | Eng. Statute Miles. | SEAPORTS. | Eng. Statute Miles. |
|---|---|---|---|
| Aberdeen and Edinboro' ... | 96 | Dublin and Liverpool ... | 126 |
| Aberdeen and London ... | 510 | Dublin and London ... ... | 823 |
| Aberdeen and Inverness ... | 140 | Dublin and Bordeaux ... | 655 |
| Aberdeen and Hull ... ... | 308 | Dublin and Glasgow ... | 223 |
| Bristol and Milford Haven ... | 127 | Dover and Dieppe ... ... | 84 |
| Bristol and Cork ... ... | 260 | Dundee and London ... | 471 |
| Bristol and Tenby ... ... | 104 | Dundee and Hull ... ... | 277 |
| Bristol and Dublin ... | 222 | Dover and Calais ... | 25 |
| Bristol and Glasgow ... | 450 | Dover and Boulogne ... ... | 30 |
| Bristol and Liverpool ... ... | 229 | Dover and Portsmouth ... | 121 |
| Bristol and Swansea ... | 73 | Exeter and Portsmouth ... | 117 |
| Bristol and Waterford ... | 219 | Edinboro' and London ... | 474 |
| Belfast and Glasgow ... | 129 | Edinboro' and Hull ... ... | 266 |
| Belfast and Dublin ... | 120 | Edinboro' and Newcastle ... | 127 |
| Belfast and Liverpool ... | 158 | Falmouth and Plymouth ... | 48 |
| Bordeaux and Nantes ... | 195 | Folkestone and Boulogne ... | 28 |
| Brest and Plymouth ... ... | 164 | Glasgow and Liverpool ... | 243 |
| Brest and Portsmouth ... | 271 | Guernsey and Southampton ... | 124 |
| Berwick and London ... ... | 395 | Guernsey and Weymouth ... | 82 |
| Brighton and Dieppe ... ... | 71 | Guernsey and Portsmouth ... | 126 |
| Brighton and Havre ... | 99 | Guernsey and Plymouth ... | 91 |
| Cherbourg and Morlaix ... | 120 | Guernsey and Jersey ... | 32 |
| Cherbourg and Havre ... | 75 | Guernsey and London ... | 310 |
| Cherbourg and Southampton ... | 100 | Glasgow and New York ... | 3400 |
| Cherbourg and Guernsey ... | 48 | Havre and Southampton ... | 102 |
| Cherbourg and Portsmouth ... | 71 | Havre and Dunkirk ... ... | 180 |
| Cork and Liverpool ... ... | 283 | Havre and Portsmouth ... | 97 |
| Cork and Plymouth ... ... | 275 | Havre and London ... | 223 |
| Cork and London ... ... | 654 | Hamburg and Leith ... | 550 |
| Cork and Milford Haven ... | 151 | Harwich and Rotterdam ... | 120 |
| Cork and Glasgow ... ... | 399 | Harwich and Antwerp ... | 135 |
| Cowes and Portsmouth ... | 12 | Hull and London ... ... | 280 |
| Cowes and Southampton ... | 13 | Hull and Rotterdam ... ... | 243 |
| Donaghadee and Portpatrick | 21 | Hull and Dunkirk ... | 235 |
| Douglas (Isle of Man) & Dublin | 88 | Hull and Hamburg ... | 442 |
| Douglas and Liverpool ... | 77 | Hull and Christiana ... | 670 |
| Douglas and Whitehaven ... | 42 | Hull and Leith ... ... | 272 |
| Dartmouth and London ... | 319 | Hull and Gottenburg ... | 594 |
| Dublin and Holyhead ... | 68 | Ilfracombe and Bristol ... | 71 |

# Table of Distances between certain Seaports in the United Kingdom and Abroad.—*Continued.*

| SEAPORTS. | Eng. Statute Miles. | SEAPORTS. | Eng. Statute Miles. |
|---|---|---|---|
| Ilfracombe and Swansea ... | 30 | London and New York ... | 3324 |
| Jersey and Plymouth | 116 | London and Philadelphia ... | 4073 |
| Jersey and Southampton ... | 131 | London and St. Petersburg ... | 1587 |
| Jersey and Weymouth | 105 | London and New Zealand ... | 15341 |
| Jersey and Granville ... ... | 34 | London and Rio Janeiro ... | 5481 |
| Jersey and St. Malo ... ... | 37 | London and Calais ... ... | 98 |
| Liverpool and Sligo ... | 354 | London and Boulogne ... | 115 |
| Liverpool and Londonderry ... | 245 | London and Margate ... | 64 |
| Liverpool and Waterford ... | 174 | London and Ramsgate ... | 71 |
| Liverpool and Whitehaven ... | 84 | London and Ostend ... ... | 122 |
| Liverpool and Dundalk ... | 145 | London and Antwerp ... | 185 |
| Liverpool and New York ... | 3016 | London and Havre ... ... | 212 |
| London and Perth ... ... | 493 | Littlehampton and Havre ... | 82 |
| London and Shields ... ... | 357 | Littlehampton and Jersey ... | 125 |
| London and Stockton ... | 343 | Marseilles and Alexandria ... | 1410 |
| London and Whitby ... | 325 | Newhaven and Dieppe ... | 64 |
| London and Scarboro' ... | 308 | Plymouth and Portsmouth ... | 154 |
| London and Boston (Lincoln) | 215 | Plymouth and Exeter ... | 80 |
| London and Yarmouth ... | 140 | Plymouth and Madeira ... | 1200 |
| London and Boulogne ... | 122 | Plymouth and Southampton | 150 |
| London and Dunkirk ... ... | 118 | Ryde and Southsea ... | 5 |
| London and Torquay ... ... | 312 | Ryde and Cowes ... | 7 |
| London and Ostend ... ... | 139 | Plymouth and Havre ... | 180 |
| London and Antwerp ... ... | 210 | Ramsgate and Calais ... ... | 32 |
| London and Rotterdam ... | 214 | Ramsgate and Boulogne ... | 43 |
| London and Hamburg ... | 482 | Ramsgate and Ostend ... | 60 |
| London and Texel ... ... | 248 | Ryde and Bournemouth ... | 27 |
| London and Southampton ... | 242 | Ryde and Southampton ... | 19 |
| London and Portsmouth ... | 225 | St. Kilda and Oban ... ... | 167 |
| London and Plymouth ... | 379 | Southampton and Gibraltar | 1160 |
| London and Amsterdam ... | 333 | Southampton and Malta ... | 2132 |
| London and Barbadoes ... | 4374 | Southampton and Alexandria | 2951 |
| London and Batavia ... ... | 13570 | Southampton and New York | 3080 |
| London and Bombay ... ... | 13018 | Southampton and Dieppe ... | 111 |
| London and Boston (U.S.) ... | 3089 | Suez to Aden ... ... ... | 1308 |
| London and Calcutta ... ... | 13934 | Suez to Madras ... ... | 3987 |
| London and Cape of Good Hope | 7567 | Suez to Calcutta ... ... | 4757 |
| London and Lima ... ... | 12339 | Suez to Bombay ... ... | 2912 |
| London and Madras ... ... | 13323 | Waterford and Milford Haven | 84 |

# WEATHER INDICATIONS.

*(Compiled for Bradshaw's Diary, from the Seaman's Almanack, Admiral Fitzroy's Weather Book, &c.)*

The following predictions of the weather, taken from careful observations, have reference generally, to our own latitude.

IT should always be remembered that the state of the air *foretells coming* weather, rather than indicates weather that is *present* (an invaluable fact too often overlooked); that the longer the time between the signs and the change foretold by them, the longer such altered weather will last; and, on the contrary, the less the time between a warning and a change, the shorter will be the continuance of such predicted weather.

If a barometer has been about its ordinary height, and is *steady*, or rising—while the thermometer falls, and dampness becomes less—north-westerly, northerly, or north-easterly wind, or less wind, less rain or snow, may be expected. On the contrary, if a fall takes place, with a rising thermometer and increased dampness, wind and rain may be expected from the south-eastward, southward, or south-westward. In winter, a considerable fall, with rather low thermometer, foretells snow. Exceptions to these rules occur.

The most dangerous shifts of wind, or the *heaviest* northerly gales, happen *soon* after the barometer *first* rises from a very low point; or, if the wind veers *gradually*, at some short time afterwards, although with a *rising* glass.

Indications of approaching change of weather, and the direction and force of winds, are shown much less by the height of the barometer than by its falling or rising.

A rapid rise of the barometer indicates unsettled weather; a slow movement of some duration, the *contrary*; as does likewise a *steady* barometer, which, when continued, and with dryness, foretells very fine weather, lasting for some time.

A rapid and considerable fall is a sign of stormy weather and rain (or snow). Alternate rising and sinking, or oscillation, always indicates unsettled and disagreeable weather.

Another remarkable peculiarity is—that the wind usually *appears* to veer, shift, or go round *with the su* (right-handed, or from left to right), and that when it does not do so, or backs, *more* wind or bad weather may be expected, instead of improvement, after a short interval.

A barometer begins to rise considerably before the conclusion of a gale, sometimes even at its commencement. Before and during the *earlier* part of settled weather it usually stands high, and is stationary, the air being dry.

Instances of fine weather with a low glass occur, however rarely, but they are always preludes to a *duration* of wind or rain.

Whether clear or cloudy, a rosy sky at sunset presages fine weather; a sickly-looking *gree ish* hue, wind and rain; a dark (or *Indian*) red, wind; a red sky in the morning, bad weather or much wind (perhaps rain); a grey sky in the morning, fine weather; a high dawn, wind; a low dawn, fair weather. A "high dawn" is when the first indications of daylight are seen above a bank of clouds. A "low dawn" is when the day breaks on or near the horizon, the first streaks of light being very low down.

Soft-looking or delicate clouds foretell fine weather, with moderate or light breezes; hard-edged, oily-looking clouds, wind. A dark, gloomy blue sky is windy, but a light, bright blue sky indicates fine weather. Generally, the *softer* clouds look, the less wind (but perhaps more rain) may be expected; and the harder, more "greasy," rolled, tufted, or ragged, the stronger the coming wind will prove. Also, a bright yellow sky at sunset presages wind, a pale yellow, wet; therefore, by the prevalence and kind of red, yellow, or other tints, the coming weather may be foretold very nearly; indeed, if aided by instruments, almost exactly.

Small inky-looking clouds foretell rain; light scud clouds, driving across heavy masses, show wind and rain; but if alone, may indicate wind only.

High upper clouds crossing the sun, moon, or stars, in a direction different from that of the lower clouds, or the wind then felt below, foretell a change of wind *toward their direction.*

After fine clear weather, the first signs in the sky of a coming change are usually light streaks, curls, wisps, or mottled patches of white distant clouds, which increase, and are followed by an overcasting of murky vapour that grows into cloudiness. This appearance, more or less oily or watery, as wind or rain will prevail, is an infallible sign.

Light, delicate, quiet tints or colours, with soft undefined forms of clouds, indicate and accompany fine weather; but unusual or gaudy hues, with hard, definitely-outlined clouds, foretell rain, and probably strong wind.

Misty clouds forming, or hanging on heights, show wind and rain coming, if they remain, increase, or descend; if they rise, or disperse, the weather will improve or become fine.

Dew is an indication of coming fine weather. Its formation never begins under an overcast sky, or when there is much wind.

Remarkable clearness of atmosphere near the horizon, distant objects, such as hills, unusually visible, or raised (by refraction), and what is called "a good hearing day," may be mentioned among the signs of wet, if not wind, to be expected.

More than usual twinkling of the stars, indistinctness or apparent multiplication of the moon's horns, haloes, fragments or pieces, as it were, of rainbows, and the rainbow itself, are more or less significant of increasing wind, if not approaching rain, with or without wind.

## Height of Towns, Places, &c., above the Sea Level.

| | Feet. | | Feet. |
|---|---|---|---|
| Aranjuez ... ... ... | 1,699 | Madrid ... ... ... | 1,974 |
| Athens (top of Parthenon) ... | 571 | Mexico ... ... ... | 7,521 |
| Berne... ... ... ... | 1,750 | Milan ... ... ... ... | 420 |
| Berlin... ... ... ... | 131 | Munich ... ... ... | 1,676 |
| Birmingham ... ... ... | 464 | Neufchatel ... ... ... | 1,384 |
| Briancon, France ... ... | 4,285 | Nottingham ... ... ... | 73 |
| Chamounix ... ... ... | 3,352 | Palace of the Escurial, Spain | 3,520 |
| Clermont ... ... ... | 1,693 | Palace of Holyrood ... ... | 118 |
| Edinboro' Castle ... ... | 434 | Paris (Observatory) ... | 213 |
| Erzeroum ... ... ... | 7,000 | Potosi ... ... ... | 13,350 |
| Folkestone (Turnpike Gate) | 575 | Pyramid (Cheops') principal.. | 475 |
| Geneva ... ... ... | 1,207 | Quito ... ... ... ... | 9,621 |
| Glurus ... ... ... | 2,750 | Radstadt ... ... ... | 2,660 |
| Greenwich (Observatory) ... | 214 | Rome (Capitol) ... ... | 151 |
| Inspruck ... ... ... | 1,693 | Rome( St. Peter's) ... ... | 518 |
| Jerusalem ... ... ... | 2,200 | Schaffhausen ... ... ... | 1,280 |
| Langres ... ... ... | 1,456 | Thiers... ... ... ... | 1,195 |
| Lamure ... ... ... | 2,919 | Thun ... ... ... ... | 1,804 |
| London (St. Paul's) ... ... | 340 | Turin (Observatory)... ... | 915 |
| Luremburg ... ... ... | 1,206 | Valladolid ... ... ... | 6,396 |

## The following places are nearly Antipodal— *i.e.*, Feet to Feet.

London with the Antipodes Island, South-east of New Zealand.

| | |
|---|---|
| Spain with New Zealand. | Lima with Siam. |
| Azores with Botany Bay. | Siberia with Falkland Islands. |
| Timbuctoo with Friendly Islands. | Nankin with Buenos Ayres. |
| Bermuda with Swan River. | Quito with Sumatra. |

| *Lakes above Sea Level.* | Feet | *Lakes below Sea Level.* | Feet |
|---|---|---|---|
| Lake Constance ... ... | 1,299 | Caspian Lake ... ... | 84 |
| Lake Geneva... ... ... | 1,229 | Lake Tiberias (Palestine) ... | 600 |
| Lake Superior ... ... | 672 | The Dead Sea ... ... | 1,312 |
| Lake Ulleswater ... ... | 318 | | |

# COMPARATIVE HEIGHTS OF SOME OF THE MOUNTAINS IN THE WORLD.

*(Compiled from Tables published by Wyld, Charing Cross.)*

| Mountain. | Country. | Feet above Sea Level. |
|---|---|---|
| Antisana | South America | 19,125 |
| Ararat | Armenia | 12,700 |
| Argentiere | Alps | 13,381 |
| Atlas | Africa | 12,500 |
| Azores | Peak in Island of | 7,016 |
| Ballon | France | 4,651 |
| Barthelemy | France | 7,365 |
| Ben Lomond | Scotland | 3,240 |
| Ben Macdui | Scotland | 4,418 |
| Ben More | Scotland | 3,870 |
| Ben Nevis | Scotland | 4,380 |
| Blanc | Switzerland | 15,630 |
| Blue Mountains | Jamaica | 7,271 |
| Breithorn | Alps | 12,793 |
| Brenner | Alps | 4,558 |
| Brocken | Germany | 3,486 |
| Cader Idris | Wales | 2,914 |
| Canijon | Alps | 9,207 |
| Cantal | France | 6,089 |
| Caro | Italy | 3,118 |
| Catopaxi | South America | 18,862 |
| Cawsand Beacon | England | 1,792 |
| Cenis | Alps | 6,773 |
| Cervin | Alps | 14,754 |
| Chamulan | Himalaya | 24,000 |
| Cheviot | England | 2,658 |
| Chimborazo | South America | 21,451 |
| Cimone | Italy | 6,971 |
| Como | Alps | 9,500 |
| Cramont | Alps | 8,958 |
| Dachstein | Alps | 9,527 |
| Dhaiban | Himalaya | 24,740 |
| Dole | France | 5,131 |
| Dunriggs | Scotland | 2,408 |

## Comparative Heights of some of the Mountains in the World.—*continued.*

| Mountain. | Country. | Feet above Sea Level. |
| --- | --- | --- |
| Egmont ... ... ... ... | New Zealand ... ... ... | 15,304 |
| Elias ... ... ... ... | North America... ... ... | 17,840 |
| Erebus ... ... ... ... | Antarctic Sea ... ... ... | 12,400 |
| Erix ... ... ... ... | Sicily ... ... ... ... | 3,891 |
| Estrella ... ... ... ... | Spain ... ... ... ... | 8,520 |
| Etna ... ... ... ... | Sicily ... ... ... ... | 10,946 |
| Fairweather ... ... ... | North America... ... ... | 14,700 |
| Ferret ... ... ... ... | Alps ... ... ... ... | 7,610 |
| Finisteraarhorn ... ... ... | Alps ... ... ... ... | 14,096 |
| Galenstock ... ... ... | Alps ... ... ... ... | 12,013 |
| Geesh ... ... ... ... | Africa ... ... ... ... | 15,000 |
| Gennaro ... ... ... ... | Italy ... ... ... ... | 4,179 |
| Genevre ... ... ... ... | Alps ... ... ... ... | 11,785 |
| Grand Vignemale ... ... | Alps ... ... ... ... | 10,820 |
| Great St. Bernard ... ... | Alps ... ... ... ... | 7,962 |
| Great Peak ... ... ... | New Mexico ... ... ... | 19,788 |
| Gries ... ... ... ... | Alps ... ... ... ... | 7,815 |
| Grimsel ... ... ... ... | Alps ... ... ... ... | 9,695 |
| Gross Glocknor ... ... ... | Alps ... ... ... ... | 12,543 |
| Gros Morne ... ... ... | Isle Bourbon ... ... ... | 9,600 |
| Hecla ... ... ... ... | Iceland ... ... ... ... | 5,000 |
| Heidelberg ... ... ... | Germany ... ... ... | 4,460 |
| Helvellyn... ... ... ... | England ... ... ... | 3,055 |
| Hood ... ... ... ... | North America... ... ... | 12,000 |
| Illimani ... ... ... ... | Peru ... ... ... ... | 24,450 |
| Ingleboro... ... ... ... | England ... ... ... | 2,361 |
| Jamnobri... ... ... ... | Himalaya ... ... ... | 25,500 |
| Jungfrauhorn ... ... ... | Alps ... ... ... ... | 13,725 |
| Krivan ... ... ... ... | Hungary ... ... ... | 8,027 |
| Kistenberg ... ... ... | Alps ... ... ... ... | 11,073 |
| Kreutzberg ... ... ... | Germany ... ... ... | 2,982 |
| Kunchinginga ... ... ... | Himalaya ... ... ... | 28,178 |
| Lanieri, Coll de- ... ... ... | Alps ... ... ... ... | 13,834 |
| Lebanon ... ... ... ... | Syria ... ... ... ... | 9,526 |
| Le Pic Blanc ... ... ... | Alps ... ... ... ... | 10,205 |

## Comparative Heights of some of the Mountains in the World.—*continued.*

| Mountain. | Country. | Feet above Sea Level. |
|---|---|---|
| Little St. Bernard | Alps | 7,188 |
| Lomnitz | Carpathians | 8,640 |
| Macgillicuddy Rocks | Ireland | 3,404 |
| Maggiore | Italy | 7,385 |
| Maladetta | France | 10,479 |
| Malvern | England | 1,444 |
| Marbore | France | 11,185 |
| Marschallhorn | Alps | 10,179 |
| Melun Rock | Alps | 11,428 |
| Mezen | France | 6,562 |
| Mourne | Ireland | 2,500 |
| Mulhacen Peak | Spain | 11,801 |
| Nepaul | Himalaya | 24,652 |
| Neplin, Mayo | Ireland | 2,634 |
| Nevado, de, Mexico | Mexico | 15,700 |
| Niewveldt | Cape of Good Hope | 10,000 |
| Oetscher | Alps | 6,377 |
| Ophir | Sumatra | 12,955 |
| Ortler Spitze | Tyrol | 14,927 |
| Orzon | Alps | 13,444 |
| Otaheite | In Island of | 10,895 |
| Otter Peak | United States | 3,955 |
| Parnassus | Spitzbergen | 3,955 |
| Pelvoux | Alps | 14,108 |
| Perdu | Pyrenees | 11,265 |
| Potosi | South America | 16,000 |
| Rathousberg | Alps | 8,715 |
| Rosa | Alps | 15,527 |
| Schneeberg | Germany | 3,423 |
| Seigne | Alps | 7,808 |
| Shap Fells | England | 3,166 |
| Simplon | Alps | 6,575 |
| Sinai | Asia | 5,000 |
| Skiddaw | England | 3,022 |
| Splugen | Alps | 6,313 |

# Comparative Heights of some of the Mountains in the World.—*continued.*

| Mountain. | Country. | Feet above Sea Level. |
|---|---|---|
| Snowdon ... ... ... ... | Wales ... ... ... ... | 3,571 |
| Snaefell ... ... ... ... | Iceland ... ... ... ... | 6,860 |
| Sneehatten ... ... ... | Norway ... ... ... ... | 8,115 |
| St. Gothard Pass .. ... ... | Alps ... ... ... ... | 6,805 |
| Steiner Alp ... ... ... | Alps ... ... ... ... | 10,941 |
| Stella ... ... ... ... | Germany ... ... ... | 11,166 |
| Sugar Loaf ... ... ... | Alps ... ... ... ... | 9,366 |
| Tadiberg ... ... ... ... | Alps ... ... ... ... | 11,832 |
| Tangai ... ... ... ... | Ural ... ... ... ... | 4,912 |
| Tende, Col de ... ... | Alps ... ... ... ... | 5,855 |
| Teneriffe Peak ... ... ... | Canaries ... ... ... | 12,358 |
| Tournette ... ... ... ... | Alps ... ... ... ... | 7,528 |
| Ventoux ... ... ... ... | Alps ... ... ... ... | 6,260 |
| Vergy ... ... ... ... | Alps ... ... ... ... | 7,495 |
| Viso ... ... ... ... | Alps ... ... ... ... | 10,051 |
| Washington or White Mountain | United States ... ... ... | 6,225 |
| Wrekin ... ... ... ... | England ... ... ... | 1,320 |

## Length of Mountain Ranges.
*(From Milner's Universal Geography.)*

| Mountain. | Country. | Miles. | Greatest Height. |
|---|---|---|---|
| | | | Feet. |
| Alps ... ... | Gulf of Genoa to Hungary ... ... | 500 | 15,750 |
| Andes ... ... | Cape Horn to Panama ... ... | 4550 | 23,200 |
| Apennines ... ... | Gulf of Genoa to extremity of Italy ... | 800 | 9,523 |
| Atlas ... ... | Atlantic Ocean to Mediterranean ... | 2000 | 11,400 |
| Balkan ... ... | Bulgaria to Black Sea ... ... | 600 | 5,596 |
| Carpathian ... ... | Upper Oder to Transylvania ... ... | 600 | 9,500 |
| Canensas ... ... | Black Sea to Caspian Sea ... ... | 700 | 18,493 |
| Grampian ... ... | Scotland ... ... ... | 100 | 4,368 |
| Himalaya ... ... | Indian Caucasus ... ... | 2000 | 28,178 |
| Lebanon ... ... | Syria to South of Dead Sea ... | 250 | 10,000 |
| Pyranees ... ... | Bay of Biscay to Mediterranean | 225 | 11,427 |
| Rocky Mountains ... | Mexico to Arctic Ocean ... ... | 3600 | 17,860 |
| Celestial Mountains | Chinese Himalaya ... ... | 1500 | 18,000 |
| Ural ... ... | Arctic Ocean to Caspian Sea ... ... | 1300 | 5,397 |

# COMPARATIVE LENGTH OF SOME OF THE PRINCIPAL RIVERS IN THE WORLD.

*(Compiled from Tables published by Wyld, Charing Cross.)*

| River. | Mouth. | Course. | Length Miles. |
|---|---|---|---|
| Amur | Pacific Ocean | Russia in Asia | 2,150 |
| Amazon | Atlantic Ocean | South America | 3,380 |
| Arkansaw | Mississippi | North America | 1,730 |
| Columbia | Pacific Ocean | North America | 900 |
| Danube | Black Sea | Germany and Austria | 1,760 |
| Dniester | Black Sea | Austria and Turkey | 710 |
| Dnieper | Black Sea | Russia | 1,140 |
| Don | Azof Sea | Russia | 1,020 |
| Douro | Atlantic Ocean | Portugal and Spain | 400 |
| Elbe | North Sea | Austria, Germany, & Prussia | 670 |
| Euphrates | Persian Gulf | Turkey in Asia | 1,900 |
| Forth | North Sea | Scotland | 115 |
| Gambia | Atlantic Ocean | Africa | 700 |
| Ganges | Bengal Bay | Hindostan | 1,550 |
| Garonne | Biscay Bay | France | 320 |
| Godavery | Indian Ocean | Hindostan | 850 |
| Guadalquivir | Atlantic Ocean | Spain | 390 |
| Hoang-ho | Pacific Ocean | China | 2,625 |
| Humber & Trent. | North Sea | England | 195 |
| Illinois | Mississippi | North America | 500 |
| Indus | Indian Ocean | Hindostan | 1,630 |
| Irwaddy | Indian Ocean | Thibet and Birman Empire | 1,260 |
| Lawrence St. | Atlantic Sea | North America | 2,340 |
| Lena | Arctic Sea | Russia in Asia | 2,370 |
| Loire | Biscay Bay | France | 545 |
| Maykau | Indian Ocean | Thibet, China, &c. | 2,090 |
| Mississippi | Mexico Gulf | North America | 1,930 |
| Missouri | Mississippi | North America | 2,310 |
| Nerbuddah | Cambay Gulf | Hindostan | 750 |
| Niemen | Baltic Sea | Russia and Prussia | 380 |
| Niger | Mediterranean | Africa | 1,000 |
| Nile | Mediterranean | Egypt, Nubia, &c. | 2,600 |
| Obe | Arctic Ocean | Chinese Tartary, & Russia | 2,550 |
| Oder | Baltic Sea | Austria and Prussia | 580 |

## Comparative Length of some of the Principal Rivers in the World.—*Continued.*

| River. | Mouth. | Course. | Length Miles. |
|---|---|---|---|
| Ohio | Mississippi | North America | 1,188 |
| Orinoco | Atlantic Ocean | South America | 1,480 |
| Parana | Plate River | South America | 1,500 |
| Plate | Atlantic Ocean | South America | 2,130 |
| Po | Adriatic Sea | Italy | 410 |
| Potomac | Chesapeake Bay | North America | 410 |
| Pruth | Danube | Turkey | 600 |
| Red River | Mississippi | North America | 1,520 |
| Rhine | North Sea | France, Germany, & Holland | 810 |
| Rhone | Mediterranean | France and Switzerland | 460 |
| Scheldt | North Sea | France and Netherlands | 170 |
| Seine | English Channel | France | 425 |
| Senegal | Atlantic Ocean | Africa | 950 |
| Severn | Bristol Channel | England | 220 |
| Shannon | Atlantic Ocean | Ireland | 200 |
| Susquehanna | Atlantic Ocean | North America | 620 |
| Tagus | Atlantic Ocean | Spain and Portugal | 550 |
| Tay | North Sea | Scotland | 120 |
| Thames | North Sea | England | 215 |
| Tigris | Euphrates | Turkey in Asia | 1,000 |
| Vistula | Baltic Sea | Austria and Prussia | 640 |
| Volga | Caspian Sea | Russia | 2,035 |
| Yang-tse-Kiang | Pacific Ocean | Thibet and China | 2,990 |

## SUPERFICIAL EXTENT OF DIFFERENT BASINS.

| Basin of River. | Geographical Sq. Miles. | Basin of River. | Geographical Sq. Miles. |
|---|---|---|---|
| Basin of the Amazon | 1,412,880 | Basin of the Oder | 33,152 |
| ,, Danube | 230,768 | ,, Po | 22,656 |
| ,, Don | 97,408 | ,, Rhine | 57,568 |
| ,, Douro | 26,208 | ,, Seine | 19,776 |
| ,, Dwina | 94,240 | ,, St. Lawrence | 997,280 |
| ,, Elbe | 44,800 | ,, Tagus | 21,712 |
| ,, Garonne | 23,088 | ,, Thames | 6,500 |
| ,, La Plate | 1,146,640 | ,, Vistula | 57,248 |
| ,, Loire | 38,048 | ,, Volga | 482,464 |
| ,, Obe | 1,040,410 | | |

Basin of a River is all the Countries over which its Branches extend.

# AREA OF PRINCIPAL LAKES IN THE WORLD.

*(From Milner's Universal Geography).*

| LAKE. | COUNTRY. | Square Miles. |
|---|---|---|
| Caspian Sea (Largest of all Lakes) | Russia ... ... about | 160,000 |
| Lake Constance ... ... ... ... | Switzerland ... ,, | 290 |
| Lake Erie ... ... ... ... ... | North America ... ,, | 11,000 |
| Lake Geneva ... ... ... ... ... | Switzerland ... ,, | 336 |
| Lake Huron ... ... ... ... ... | North America ... ,, | 25,000 |
| Loch Lomond ... ... ... ... | Scotland ... ,, | ... 45 |
| Lake Lucerne ... ... ... ... | Switzerland... ... ,, | 99 |
| Lake Maggiore ... ... ... ... | Italy ... ... ... ,, | 152 |
| Lake Michigan ... ... ... ... | North America ... ,, | 25,000 |
| Lough Neagh ... ... ... ... | Ireland ... ,, | 158 |
| Lake Ontario ... ... ... ... | North America ... ,, | 10,000 |
| Lake Onega ... ... ... ... ... | North America ... ,, | 43,000 |
| Lake Superior ... ... ... ... | Switzerland ... ,, | 3,280 |
| Lake Wener ... ... ... ... ... | Russia ... ... ... ,, | 2,136 |
| Lake We ter ... ... ... ... ... | Sweden ... ... ,, | 832 |
| Lake Zurich ... ... ... ... ... | Sweden ... ... ,, | 76 |

## AREA OF EUROPEAN SEAS.

| | | Sq. Miles. |
|---|---|---|
| Adriatic Sea ... ... ... ... ... about | | 62,900 |
| Baltic Sea (with Gulfs) ... ... ... ... ,, | | 134,200 |
| Black Sea and Sea of Azof ... ... ... ... ,, | | 181,000 |
| Egean Sea ... ... ... ... ... ,, | | 73,400 |
| English Channel ... ... ... ... ... ,, | | 28,200 |
| Irish Sea and St. George's Channel ... ... ... ,, | | 25,900 |
| Marmora Sea of ... ... ... ... ... ,, | | 3,800 |
| Mediterrannean Sea ... ... ... ... ... ,, | | 867,000 |
| North Sea and German Ocean ... ... ... ,, | | 244,000 |
| White Sea ... ... ... ... ... ,, | | 38,600 |

## OCEANS.

| | | Square Miles. |
|---|---|---|
| The Atlantic Ocean ... ... ... ... about | | 25,000,000 |
| The Indian Ocean ... ... ... ... ,, | | 18,000,000 |
| The Pacific Ocean ... ... ... ... ,, | | 50,000,000 |

## CANALS, RIVERS, &c.

| | |
|---|---|
| Canals in the United States ... ... ... ... | about 2,500 miles. |
| Canals in England ... ... ... ... ... | ,, 2,800 ,, |
| Canals in Ireland ... ... ... ... ... | ,, 300 ,, |
| First Canal made in England ... ... ... | about the year 1134 |
| Last do. do. ... ... ... ... | ,, ,, 1831 |
| Rivers in England (navigable) ... ... ... | about 2,500 miles. |
| Ditto in Ireland ,, ... ... ... | ,, 210 ,, |
| Coast Line of Great Britain ... ... ... | about 3,112 miles. |

# MILITARY, NAVAL, AND MERCANTILE MARINE STRENGTH OF PRINCIPAL COUNTRIES OF THE WORLD.

*(Compiled and arranged for Bradshaw's Diary from " Martin's Statesman's Year Book.")*

| COUNTRY. | ARMY. Standing Army. (Peace footing.) No. Men. | NAVAL FORCE. War Ships of all descriptions (Steam & Sail). | Guns. | Men, including Marines | MERCANTILE NAVY. Ships. | Tonnage. |
|---|---|---|---|---|---|---|
| Argentine Republic ......... | 30,567 | 17 | — | — | — | — |
| Austria... ... ... ... ... | 269,103 | 59 | 784 | 14,331 | 9,643 | 331,287 |
| Belgium ... ... ... ... | 73,718 | 7 | — | — | 112 | 39,729 |
| Baden (South Germany) ... | 14,919 | — | — | — | — | — |
| Bavaria (South Germany)... | 81,337 | — | — | — | — | — |
| Brazil ... ... ... ... ... | 33,575 | 61 | — | 14,909 | — | — |
| Bremen (North Germany)... | — | — | — | — | 305 | 253,286 |
| Canada... ... ... ... ... | — | — | — | — | 5,477 | 755,502 |
| Chili ... ... ... ... ... | 5,300 | 5 | — | — | — | — |
| China ... ... ... ... | 600,000 | — | — | — | — | — |
| Denmark ... ... ... ... | 42,317 | 35 | 387 | 1,423 | 3,736 | 172,460 |
| Egypt ... ... ... ... | 14,000 | 74 | — | — | — | — |
| Finland ... ... ... ... | — | — | — | — | 532 | 160,000 |
| France ... ... ... ... ... | 404,192 | 480 | 2,750 | 43,080 | 15,637 | 1,042,811 |
| Great Britain and Ireland... | 201,641 | 466 | — | 30,000 | 21,777 | 5,493,708 |
| Greece ... ... ... ... ... | 31,300 | 32 | — | — | — | — |
| Hamburg and Hanse Towns | — | — | — | — | 509 | 80,837 |
| Hesse Darmstadt (S. Germ.) | 11,510 | — | — | — | — | — |
| Italy ... ... ... ... ... | 189,541 | 106 | 1,468 | 22,789 | 15,728 | 678,603 |
| Japan ... ... ... ... ... | 80,000 | 12 | 49 | — | — | — |
| Mecklenburg (N. Germany) | — | — | — | — | 419 | 151,740 |
| Netherlands... ... ... ... | 91,028 | 150 | 936 | 9,269 | 2,203 | 269,338 |
| Norway ... ... ... ... | 12,150 | 156 | 500 | 4,000 | 5,407 | 352,949 |
| Papal States... ... ... ... | 9,588 | — | — | — | — | — |
| Paraguay ... ... ... ... | 60,000 | 39 | — | — | — | — |
| Persia ... ... ... ... ... | 30,000 | — | — | — | — | — |
| Peru ... ... ... ... ... | 16,008 | 7 | — | — | — | — |
| Portugal ... ... ... ... | 18,185 | 34 | 294 | 2,832 | 829 | 87,953 |
| Prussia and North Germany | 208,576 | 99 | 539 | 3,557 | 1,443 | 187,308 |
| Russia ... ... ... ... ... | 812,096 | 292 | 2,387 | 64,021 | 1,927 | 205,759 |
| Saxony (North Germany)... | 25,400 | — | — | — | — | — |
| Spain ... ... ... ... ... | 151,668 | 109 | 1,055 | 22,087 | 4,840 | 367,790 |
| Sweden... ... ... ... ... | 144,010 | 18 | 76 | 34,578 | 1,248 | 66,423 |
| Switzerland... ... ... ... | 339,926 | — | — | — | — | — |
| Turkey... ... ... ... ... | 459,360 | 40 | — | — | — | — |
| United States ... ... ... | 50,000 | 278 | 2,351 | 13,600 | 17,490 | 4,310,778 |
| Uruguay ... ... ... ... | 22,800 | — | — | — | — | — |
| Wurtemburg ... ... ... | 10,371 | — | — | — | — | — |

# TABLE OF SOME OF THE PRINCIPAL BRIDGES IN THE UNITED KINGDOM—(Dates of Opening).

*(Compiled for Bradshaw's Diary.)*

| | |
|---|---|
| Queen's Bridge, Dublin | 1768 |
| Blackfriars Bridge (Old Bridge) | November 19, 1769 |
| Exeter Bridge | 1778 |
| Coalbrook Dale Bridge | 1779 |
| Bailey Bridge, Manchester | 1785 |
| Kew Bridge | September 23, 1789 |
| Sarah Bridge, Dublin | 1791 |
| Carlisle Bridge, Dublin | 1794 |
| Bristol Bridge | 1806 |
| Vauxhall Bridge | June 4, 1816 |
| Waterloo Bridge | June 18, 1817 |
| Southwark Bridge | March 23, 1819 |
| Sunderland Bridge | March 25, 1819 |
| Union Bridge at Berwick-on-Tweed | July, 1820 |
| New Brunswick Bridge, Manchester | 1820 |
| Menai Straits Suspension Bridge | January 30, 1826 |
| Conway Suspension Bridge | 1826 |
| Hammersmith Suspension Bridge | October 6, 1827 |
| Gloucester Bridge | 1827 |
| London Bridge | August 1, 1831 |
| Dee Bridge, Chester | 1833 |
| Royal Border Bridge, Berwick-on-Tweed | 1846 |
| High Level Bridge, Newcastle-on-Tyne | 1846 |
| Conway Tubular Bridge | 1848 |
| Britannia Tubular Bridge (Menai Straits) | 1850 |
| Chepstow Tubular Bridge | 1852 |
| Rochester Bridge | August, 1856 |
| Chelsea Suspension Bridge | 1858 |
| Rochester Railway Bridge | March, 1858 |
| Saltash Tubular Bridge | May 2, 1859 |
| Westminster New Bridge | May 24, 1862 |
| Lambeth and Westminster Suspension Bridge | 1862 |
| Charing Cross Railway Bridge | December 2, 1863 |
| Blackfriars Railway Bridge | October 6, 1864 |
| Clifton Suspension Bridge | December 8, 1864 |
| Victoria Railway Bridge, Pimlico | February, 1865 |
| Cannon Street Railway Bridge | September 1, 1866 |
| | |
| Brighton Chain Pier | 1823 |
| Thames Tunnel | March 25, 1843 |

# TABLES OF CALCULATION.

## TABLE OF EXPENSES, INCOME, OR WAGES.

| Per Year. | Per Month | Per Week. | Per Day. | Per Year. | Per Month. | Per Week. | Per Day. |
|---|---|---|---|---|---|---|---|
| £ | £ s. d. | £ s. d. | s. d. | £ | £ s. d. | £ s. d. | £ s. d. |
| 1 | 0 1 8 | 0 0 4½ | 0 0¾ | 20 | 1 13 4 | 0 7 8 | 0 1 1¼ |
| 2 | 0 3 4 | 0 0 9¼ | 0 1¼ | 30 | 2 10 0 | 0 11 6 | 0 1 7¾ |
| 3 | 0 5 0 | 0 1 1¾ | 0 2 | 40 | 3 6 8 | 0 15 4 | 0 2 2¼ |
| 4 | 0 6 8 | 0 1 6½ | 0 2¾ | 50 | 4 3 4 | 0 19 2 | 0 2 9 |
| 5 | 0 8 4 | 0 1 11 | 0 3¼ | 60 | 5 0 0 | 1 3 0¾ | 0 3 3½ |
| 6 | 0 10 0 | 0 2 3½ | 0 4 | 70 | 5 16 8 | 1 6 10¾ | 0 3 10 |
| 7 | 0 11 8 | 0 2 8¼ | 0 4½ | 80 | 6 13 4 | 1 10 8¾ | 0 4 4¾ |
| 8 | 0 13 4 | 0 3 0¾ | 0 5¼ | 90 | 7 10 0 | 1 14 6¾ | 0 4 11¼ |
| 9 | 0 15 0 | 0 3 5½ | 0 6 | 100 | 8 6 8 | 1 18 4½ | 0 5 5¾ |
| 10 | 0 16 8 | 0 3 10 | 0 6½ | 200 | 16 13 4 | 3 16 9 | 0 11 0 |
| 11 | 0 18 4 | 0 4 2¾ | 0 7¼ | 300 | 25 0 0 | 5 15 1 | 0 16 5 |
| 12 | 1 0 0 | 0 4 7¼ | 0 8 | 400 | 33 6 8 | 7 13 5 | 1 1 11 |
| 13 | 1 1 8 | 0 4 11¾ | 0 8½ | 500 | 41 13 4 | 9 11 9 | 1 7 5 |
| 14 | 1 3 4 | 0 5 4½ | 0 9¼ | 600 | 50 0 0 | 11 10 2 | 1 2 11 |
| 15 | 1 5 0 | 0 5 9 | 0 9¾ | 700 | 58 6 8 | 13 8 6 | 1 18 4 |
| 16 | 1 6 8 | 0 6 1½ | 0 10½ | 800 | 66 13 4 | 15 6 10 | 2 3 10 |
| 17 | 1 8 4 | 0 6 6½ | 0 11¼ | 900 | 75 0 0 | 17 5 2 | 2 9 4 |
| 18 | 1 10 0 | 0 6 10¾ | 0 11¾ | 1000 | 83 6 8 | 19 3 7 | 2 14 10 |
| 19 | 1 11 8 | 0 7 3½ | 1 0½ | | | | |

The Months in the above Table are calculated at Twelve Months to the Year. If the Yearly Wages be Guineas instead of Pounds, for each Guinea add One Penny to each Month or One Farthing to each Week.

## INTEREST TABLE FOR £100,

*At* 3, 3½, 4, 4½, *and* 5 *per Cent.*

| Days. | 3 per cent. | 3½ per cent. | 4 per cent. | 4½ per cent. | 5 per cent. | Days. | 3 per cent. | 3½ per cent. | 4 per cent. | 4½ per cent. | 5 per cent. |
|---|---|---|---|---|---|---|---|---|---|---|---|
| | s. d. | s. d. | s. d. | s. d. | s. d. | | £ s. d. | £ s. d. | £ s. d. | £ s. d. | £ s. d. |
| 1 | 0 1¾ | 0 2¼ | 0 2½ | 0 2¾ | 0 3¼ | 30 | 0 4 11 | 0 5 9 | 0 6 6¾ | 0 7 4¼ | 0 8 2½ |
| 2 | 0 3¾ | 0 4½ | 0 5¼ | 0 5¾ | 0 6½ | 40 | 0 6 6¾ | 0 7 8 | 0 8 9 | 0 9 10¼ | 0 10 11½ |
| 3 | 0 5¾ | 0 6¾ | 0 7¾ | 0 8¾ | 0 9¾ | 50 | 0 8 2½ | 0 9 7 | 0 10 11½ | 0 12 3¾ | 0 13 8¼ |
| 4 | 0 7¾ | 0 9 | 0 10½ | 0 11¾ | 1 1 | 60 | 0 9 10¼ | 0 11 6 | 0 13 1¾ | 0 14 9½ | 0 16 5 |
| 5 | 0 9¾ | 0 11½ | 1 1 | 1 2¾ | 1 4¼ | 70 | 0 11 6 | 0 13 5 | 0 15 4 | 0 17 3 | 0 19 2 |
| 6 | 0 11¾ | 1 1¾ | 1 3¾ | 1 5¾ | 1 7½ | 80 | 0 13 1¾ | 0 15 4 | 0 17 6¼ | 0 19 8½ | 1 1 11 |
| 7 | 1 1¾ | 1 4 | 1 6¼ | 1 8½ | 1 11 | 90 | 0 14 9½ | 0 17 3 | 0 19 8¾ | 1 2 2¾ | 1 4 7¾ |
| 8 | 1 3¾ | 1 6¼ | 1 9 | 1 11½ | 2 2¼ | 100 | 0 16 5¼ | 0 19 2 | 1 1 11 | 1 4 8 | 1 7 4¾ |
| 9 | 1 5¾ | 1 8½ | 1 11½ | 2 2½ | 2 5½ | 200 | 1 12 10½ | 1 18 4¼ | 2 3 10 | 2 9 3¾ | 2 14 9½ |
| 10 | 1 7½ | 1 11 | 2 2¼ | 2 5½ | 2 8¾ | 300 | 2 9 3¾ | 2 17 6¼ | 3 5 9 | 3 14 0 | 4 2 2¼ |
| 20 | 3 3¼ | 3 10 | 4 4½ | 4 11 | 5 5¾ | | | | | | |

## TABLE TO ADD UP EXPENSES.

| By Day. | By Week. | By Mon. | By Year. | By Day. | By Week. | By Mon. | By Year. |
|---|---|---|---|---|---|---|---|
| £ s. d. | £ s. d. | £ s. d. | £ s. d. | £ s. d. | £ s. d. | £ s. d. | £ s. d. |
| 0 0 1 | 0 0 7 | 0 2 4 | 1 10 5 | 0 6 0 | 2 2 0 | 8 8 0 | 109 10 0 |
| 0 0 2 | 0 1 2 | 0 4 8 | 3 0 10 | 0 7 0 | 2 9 0 | 9 16 0 | 127 15 0 |
| 0 0 3 | 0 1 9 | 0 7 0 | 4 11 3 | 0 8 0 | 2 16 0 | 11 4 0 | 146 0 0 |
| 0 0 4 | 0 2 4 | 0 9 4 | 6 1 8 | 0 9 0 | 3 3 0 | 12 12 0 | 164 5 0 |
| 0 0 5 | 0 2 11 | 0 11 8 | 7 12 1 | 0 10 0 | 3 10 0 | 14 0 0 | 182 10 0 |
| 0 0 6 | 0 3 6 | 0 14 0 | 9 2 6 | 0 11 0 | 3 17 0 | 15 8 0 | 200 15 0 |
| 0 0 7 | 0 4 1 | 0 16 4 | 10 12 11 | 0 12 0 | 4 4 0 | 16 16 0 | 219 0 0 |
| 0 0 8 | 0 4 8 | 0 18 8 | 12 3 4 | 0 13 0 | 4 11 0 | 18 4 0 | 237 5 0 |
| 0 0 9 | 0 5 3 | 1 1 0 | 13 13 9 | 0 14 0 | 4 18 0 | 19 12 0 | 255 10 0 |
| 0 0 10 | 0 5 10 | 1 3 4 | 15 4 2 | 0 15 0 | 5 5 0 | 21 0 0 | 273 15 0 |
| 0 0 11 | 0 6 5 | 1 5 8 | 16 14 7 | 0 16 0 | 5 12 0 | 22 8 0 | 292 0 0 |
| 0 1 0 | 0 7 0 | 1 8 0 | 18 5 0 | 0 17 0 | 5 19 0 | 23 16 0 | 310 5 0 |
| 0 2 0 | 0 14 0 | 2 16 0 | 36 10 0 | 0 18 0 | 6 6 0 | 25 4 0 | 328 10 0 |
| 0 3 0 | 1 1 0 | 4 4 0 | 54 15 0 | 0 19 0 | 6 13 0 | 26 12 0 | 346 15 0 |
| 0 4 0 | 1 8 0 | 5 12 0 | 73 0 0 | 1 0 0 | 7 0 0 | 28 0 0 | 365 0 0 |
| 0 5 0 | 1 15 0 | 7 0 0 | 91 5 0 | | | | |

# TABLE FOR CALCULATING SPEED ON LAND.

*(Compiled and arranged for Bradshaw's Diary.)*

DIRECTIONS.—After having ascertained the time of any moving object (say "Train," "Horse," &c.) effecting either of the mile-runs from post to post, seek this number in the time column, and even therewith, will be found the travelling or moving speed per hour.

| TIME. Min. | Sec. | Miles per Hour. | TIME. Min. | Sec. | Miles per Hour. | TIME. Min. | Sec | Miles per Hour. | TIME. Min. | Sec. | Miles per Hour. |
|---|---|---|---|---|---|---|---|---|---|---|---|
| 1 | 0 | 60 | 1 | 16 | 47 | 1 | 46 | 34 | 2 | 52 | 21 |
| 1 | 1 | 59 | 1 | 18 | 46 | 1 | 49 | 33 | 3 | 0 | 20 |
| 1 | 2 | 58 | 1 | 20 | 45 | 1 | 52 | 32 | 3 | 10 | 19 |
| 1 | 3 | 57 | 1 | 22 | 44 | 1 | 56 | 31 | 3 | 20 | 18 |
| 1 | 4 | 56 | 1 | 24 | 43 | 2 | 0 | 30 | 3 | 32 | 17 |
| 1 | 5 | 55 | 1 | 26 | 42 | 2 | 4 | 29 | 3 | 44 | 16 |
| 1 | 6 | 54 | 1 | 28 | 41 | 2 | 8 | 28 | 4 | 0 | 15 |
| 1 | 7 | 53 | 1 | 30 | 40 | 2 | 14 | 27 | 4 | 16 | 14 |
| 1 | 8 | 52 | 1 | 32 | 39 | 2 | 18 | 26 | 4 | 36 | 13 |
| 1 | 10 | 51 | 1 | 35 | 38 | 2 | 24 | 25 | 5 | 0 | 12 |
| 1 | 12 | 50 | 1 | 37 | 37 | 2 | 30 | 24 | 5 | 28 | 11 |
| 1 | 13 | 49 | 1 | 40 | 36 | 2 | 36 | 23 | 6 | 0 | 10 |
| 1 | 15 | 48 | 1 | 43 | 35 | 2 | 44 | 22 | 6 | 40 | 9 |

# TABLE FOR CALCULATING THE SPEED OF SHIPS.
## MEASURED MILE SPEED TABLE.

| Min. | SECONDS. 0 | 3 | 6 | 9 | 12 | 15 | 18 | 21 | 24 | 27 |
|---|---|---|---|---|---|---|---|---|---|---|
| | NAUTICAL MILES PER HOUR. | | | | | | | | | |
| 3 | 20·000 | 19·672 | 19·355 | 19·047 | 18·750 | 18·461 | 18·181 | 17·910 | 17·647 | 17·391 |
| 4 | 15·000 | 14·815 | 14·634 | 14·457 | 14·285 | 14·118 | 13·953 | 13·793 | 13·636 | 13·483 |
| 5 | 12·000 | 11·880 | 11·764 | 11·650 | 11·538 | 11·428 | 11·321 | 11·215 | 11·111 | 11·009 |
| 6 | 10·000 | 9·917 | 9·830 | 9·756 | 9·677 | 9·600 | 9·524 | 9·448 | 9·375 | 9·302 |
| 7 | 8·571 | 8·510 | 8·450 | 8·391 | 8·333 | 8·275 | 8·219 | 8·163 | 8·108 | 8·059 |

| Min. | SECONDS. 30 | 33 | 36 | 39 | 42 | 45 | 48 | 51 | 54 | 57 |
|---|---|---|---|---|---|---|---|---|---|---|
| | NAUTICAL MILES PER HOUR. | | | | | | | | | |
| 3 | 17·143 | 16·901 | 16·667 | 16·438 | 16·216 | 16·000 | 15·789 | 15·58 4 | 15·384 | 15·190 |
| 4 | 13·333 | 13·186 | 13·043 | 12·903 | 12·766 | 12·631 | 12·500 | 12·371 | 12·245 | 12·121 |
| 5 | 10·909 | 10·810 | 10·714 | 10 619 | 10·526 | 10·434 | 10·345 | 10·256 | 10·169 | 10·084 |
| 6 | 9·230 | 9·160 | 9·090 | 9·022 | 8·955 | 8 889 | 8·823 | 8·759 | 8·695 | 8·633 |
| 7 | 8·000 | 7·947 | 7·895 | 7·843 | 7·792 | 7·741 | 7·692 | 7·643 | 7·595 | 7·547 |

# ELECTRIC TELEGRAPH INFORMATION.

SUGGESTIONS TO THE PUBLIC FOR TRANSMITTING MESSAGES.

Write as plainly as possible—Express figures by words—Divide your sentences—Give full address—Run no risk of errors—Note the time you give in your message for transmission—Make your message as plain and concise as possible.

Have important messages repeated, for which half rates are charged.

INSURED MESSAGES.—The accuracy of important Telegraph Messages to the Continent can be insured for any sum from £100 up to £1000, at the rate of about 1 per cent *charge for messages*. The uniform charge for telegrams is one shilling for messages not exceeding twenty words. Delivery and porterage is charged for beyond (say) half-a-mile from the Telegraph Station.

The Telegraph Stations in principal towns are open day and night; but at Country Railway Stations they are, as a rule, closed about 7 p.m. or 8 p.m.

## Telegraph Companies in the United Kingdom.

|  | Miles in Length. | Miles of Wires. | No. of Telegraph Stations open to Public. | No. of Instruments used. | No. of Public Messages sent. |
|---|---|---|---|---|---|
| Electric and International... | 9,306 | 45,044 | 1,180 | 4,489 | 2,196,046 |
| British and Irish Magnetic... | 4,401 | 18,668 | 491 | 1,042 | 1,251,265 |
| South Eastern................ | 323 | 3,064 | 104 | 142 | 88,711 |
| London Brighton & S. Coast | 241 | 688 | 57 | 159 | 66,523 |
| London District ............. | 123 | 471 | 83 | 192 | 316,272 |
| United Kingdom............. | 1,672 | 9,506 | 125 | 172 | 743,870 |
| TOTAL........ | 16,066 | 77,441 | 2,040 | 6,196 | 4,662,687 |

## Length of Telegraph Lines in different Countries.

| COUNTRIES. | MILES. | COUNTRIES. | MILES. |
|---|---|---|---|
| Belgium    ...    ...    ... | 1,089 | Russia    ...    ...    ... | 22,992 |
| Canada    ...    ...    ... | 5,050 | Sweden    ...    ...    ... | 3,507 |
| France    ...    ...    ... | 18,964 | Switzerland    ...    ... | 2,160 |
| Germany    ...    ...    ... | 28,347 | Turkey    ...    ...    ... | 8,665 |
| Great Britain & Ireland    ... | 16,297 | United States    ...    ... | 52,957 |
| Italy    ...    ...    ... | 8,216 | Victoria    ...    ...    ... | 3,110 |

Total Length of Land Telegraph Wires in the World, about 180,000 miles.

## Submarine Cables.

| | |
|---|---|
| Dover and Calais ...    ...    ...    ...    ...    ... | Laid 13th November, 1851 |
| Holyhead and Dublin    ...    ...    ...    ...    ,, | ———— 1852 |
| Dover and Ostend ...    ...    ...    ...    ...    ,, | May, 1853 |
| Portpatrick and Donaghadee    ...    ...    ...    ,, | May, 1853 |
| England and America (first attempt)    ...    ...    ,, | 5th August, 1858 |
| Aden and Suez    ...    ...    ...    ...    ...    ,, | May, 1859 |
| Malta and Alexandria    ...    ...    ...    ...    ,, | September, 1861 |
| England and America    ...    ...    ...    ...    ,, | 27th July, 1866 |

Length of Two Atlantic Cables ...    ...    ...    ...    ...    4,369
Do.    of Submarine Cables    ..    ...    ...    ...    ...    6,000

# POSTAL REGULATIONS.

*(Compiled for Bradshaw's Diary.)*

The following are the Regulations for the transmission of letters &c, in the United Kingdom, and between the United Kingdom and Abroad.

RATES OF POSTAGE FOR LETTERS.—Inland letters to any part of the United Kingdom (the Channel Islands included), if not exceeding ½ oz., are charged 1d.

Exceeding ½ oz., but not exceeding 1 oz. 2d.

| " | 1 oz., | " | " | 1½ oz. 3d. |
| " | 1½ oz., | " | " | 2 oz. 4d. |
| " | 2 oz., | " | " | 2½ oz. 5d. |
| " | 2½ oz., | " | " | oz. 6d. |

and so on, one penny being charged for every additional half ounce or fraction. Unstamped or unpaid letters are charged double postage on delivery ; those insufficiently stamped, double the amount of such insufficiency. No limit exists to the weight of paid letters, but no Inland Letter must exceed 2½ inches any way.

UNPAID LETTERS.—Persons sending Letters by Post unpaid, which from any cause cannot be delivered, are liable to pay the Postage so charged, under the 3 and 4 of Victoria, cap. 96, and the 10 and 11 of Victoria, cap. 85 ; and under the 1 of Victoria, cap. 36, may be recovered with costs, by summary process before a Magistrate.

Letters re-directed are subject to a second Postage, at the rate charged for Prepaid Letters.

DELIVERY OF LETTERS IN LONDON.—There are twelve deliveries daily—seven within a circle of four miles, and the remainder for longer distances ; the first at 7·30 a.m., the second at 9 a.m., and every hour until 7.45 p.m. There is no delivery in the London district on Sundays.

LONDON POSTAL DISTRICTS.—London and the Suburban Villages, &c., are divided into Eight Postal Districts. The following are the names of the Districts, with their abbreviations, viz. :—

| | | | | |
|---|---|---|---|---|
| Eastern | ..............................E. | | Northern | .........................N. |
| East Central | ...................E.C. | | North Western | ...........N.W. |
| Western | ............................W. | | South Eastern | ...............S.E. |
| West Central | ..............W.C. | | South Western | ...............S.W. |

REGISTERED LETTERS.—Inland, Colonial, and Ship Letters can be registered on payment of 4d. in addition to the postage.

*Registered Letters for France*, and Countries through France, must be prepaid with double the amount of the ordinary postage ; and those for Prussia, and Countries through Prussia, are liable to a Registration fee of 4d., which, with the Postage, must be paid in advance. Registered Letters for the Night Mails must be posted half an hour before the ordinary Letters, but are received at the General Post Office, and at the Chief District and Branch Offices in London, up to 6 p.m., on payment of an additional fee of 4d.

SOLDIERS' OR SEAMEN'S LETTERS are subject to a postage of 1d., if prepaid and under ½ an oz. ; by private ship, 1d., the gratuity in addition must be paid. Letters from Abroad, sent by or addressed to Soldiers or Seamen, when unpaid, are charged 2d. If sent to or through a Foreign country, they are liable to Foreign rates in addition, but to no further charge upon re-direction. Letters from Soldiers or Seamen to the United States are subject to the United States rate of 2½d. in addition to the usual reduced rate, the whole to be paid in advance when posted in this country.

NEWSPAPERS AND BOOKS.—Newspapers (Stamped) sent by Post, must be made up in covers open at the sides, and have the impressed Stamp visible, and no marks or writing (besides the address) thereon, or anything enclosed, or it subjects them to Letter Postage. British Newspapers, when duly stamped, are forwarded free throughout the United Kingdom (except those delivered within three miles of the place where posted, which are charged 1d.). Unstamped Newspapers, if weighing under 4 oz., may be forwarded between places in the United Kingdom by affixing 1d. Postage Stamp. For places Abroad the Impressed Stamp is valueless, as the Postage must be prepaid by Postage Labels. Newspapers for Foreign parts and Colonies, if posted later than 15 days after date of publication, are charged Letter Postage.

BOOKS, &c.—Printed Books, Pamphlets, Magazines, &c., whether British, Foreign, or Colonial, may be forwarded by Post between places in the United Kingdom (made up in the same manner as Newspapers), if prepaid in stamps, at the following rates :—

| | | |
|---|---|---|
| Under 4 oz. | ............................................. | 1d. |
| " 8 oz. | ............................................. | 2d. |
| " 16 oz. | ............................................. | 4d. |
| " 24 oz. | ............................................. | 6d. |
| " 32 oz. | ............................................. | 8d. |

and 2d. for every additional 8 oz., or any less weight ; no Parcel to exceed 2½ inches any

way, but may contain more than one book, &c. They must be posted half an hour before the first collection of letters, and not in Pillar Boxes.

A Book Packet may contain any writing not of the nature of a Letter, any number of separate Books or other Publications, Prints, or Maps, and any quantity of Paper, Parchment, or Vellum.

FOREIGN AND COLONIAL MAILS.—The Mails are made up as follows :—

Australia, New South Wales, New Zealand, Queensland, and Tasmania, *via* Southampton, 20th, Morn., 6d. ; *via* Marseilles, 26th, Even., 10d.

Belgium and Continent of Europe, *via* Belgium, daily.

Canada, Thursday, E., 6d. ; Saturday, E., *via* United States, 8d.

Cape Coast Castle and Sierra Leone, 23rd, E., 6d.

Cape of Good Hope, 9th, E., 1s.

Ceylon, *via* Marseilles, 10th and 26th, E., 10d. ; *via* Southampton, 4th and 20th, M., 6d

China, *via* Marseilles, 10th and 20th, E., 1s. 4d. ; *via* Southampton, 4th and 20th, M., 1s.

Egypt, *via* Marseilles, 3rd, 10th, 18th, and 26th, E., 6d. under $\frac{1}{4}$ oz.; *via* Southampton, 4th, 12th, 20th and 27th, M., 6d. under $\frac{1}{2}$ oz.

France and the Continent of Europe, *via* France, twice daily, 4d. under $\frac{1}{2}$ oz.

Gibraltar, *via* France, M. and E., 6d. under $\frac{1}{4}$ oz.; *via* Southampton, 4th, 12th, 20th, and 27th, M., 6d. under $\frac{1}{2}$ oz.

India, *via* Marseilles, 3rd, 10th, 18th, 26th, E., 10d. ; *via* Southampton, 4th, 12th, 20th, and 27th, M., 6d. ; Malta, *via* Southampton, 4th, 12th, 20th, and 27th, M., 6d., under $\frac{1}{2}$ oz.

Mauritius, *via* Southampton, 20th, M., 6d. ; *via* Marseilles, 26th, E., 10d.

New Brunswick, and Nova Scotia, alt. Sat., E., 6d., or *via* United States.

Newfoundland and Prince Edward Island, alt. Sat., E., 6d.

United States, every Saturday evening and Wednesday evening, 1s.

Vancouver's Island and British Columbia, every Sat., E., 1s,; *via* St. Thomas and Panama, 2nd and 17th, M., 2s. 4d.

West Indias (British), 2nd and 7th, M., 1s.

FOREIGN POSTAGE. The rates of Foreign Postage varying with every country, and according to different scales of weight, it has been found impossible to give any table within our limits. In the "Postal Guide," the information occupies altogether above twenty-five pages. It may be enough to state here, that to all the British Colonies and Possessions, when sent direct (*i. e.*, not through Marseilles to Alexandria), and to the United States of America, the lowest rate of payment covers half an ounce. To all European countries, the lowest rate is for a quarter of an ounce only, as well as for letters sent through them to British Possessions. To some parts of South America also, the lowest scale is for half an ounce, but only to the port of discharge, whence there is an additional inland postage. Book parcels and unstamped newspapers are carried to the British Possessions and delivered, at threepence for four ounces ; and the same rate is charged to other places, with some few exceptions, but only to the port of discharge. An additional penny for each four ounces is charged when sent to British Possessions through France, and to some places the latter rate of postage is charged. To Prussia no letter can be conveyed by post weighing more than $1\frac{1}{2}$ oz.

MONEY ORDERS.—Money Orders are granted and paid at every Post Town in the United Kingdom, at a charge of 3d. for sums not above £2 ; 6d. not above £5 ; 9d. not above £7 ; and 1s. not above £10, which is the highest sum for which a single Order is granted.

Money Orders drawn on London are payable only at the Chief Office, between 10 and 4, except on Saturdays, and then between 10 and 1.

Payment of a Money Order must be obtained before the end of the second month from the date when issued, or a fresh commission is charged, and no Order is paid after twelve clear months.

Money Orders are granted and paid in London, within the Town limits, between 10 and 4, and in the Suburban districts, from 9 till 6 daily.

The receivers are not obliged to sell Stamps, or receive Registered Letters, or attend to any other official business, after 8 p.m.

## Postal Statistics from Postmaster-General's Report.

Letters delivered in the United Kingdom, for year 1867, about 775,000,000.
Averaging 144 Letters to each inhabited house in the United Kingdom.
Book packets by post in the United Kingdom .........about 102,000,000.

# LONDON CAB FARES AND REGULATIONS.

*(Compiled for Bradshaw's Diary.)*

The following abstract of the various Laws relating to Hackney Carriages has been drawn up for the guidance of drivers and of the public by the Chief Commissioner of Police of the Metropolis.

Fares are according to distance or time, *at the option of the hirer expressed at the commencement of the hiring ;* if not otherwise expressed, the fare to be paid according to distance.

No driver is compellable to hire his carriage for a fare according to time, at any time after eight o'clock in the evening, and before six o'clock in the morning.

An agreement to pay more than legal fare is not binding, any sum paid beyond the fare may be recovered back.

Driver not to charge more than the sum agreed on for driving a distance, although such distance be exceeded by the driver.

If the driver agree beforehand to take any sum less than the proper fare, the penalty for exacting or demanding more than the sum agreed upon is 40s.

Driver may demand a reasonable sum as a deposit, from persons hiring and requiring him to wait, over and above the fare to which the driver is entitled for driving thither. If driver refuse to wait, or go away before expiration of time for which deposit shall be sufficient compensation, or if driver shall refuse to account for such deposit, the penalty is 40s.

Hirer refusing to pay the fare, or for any damage and compensation for loss of time, may be committed to prison.

The number of persons to be carried shall be distinctly marked on such carriage, and the driver shall, if required by the hirer, carry by such carriage the number of persons marked thereon, or any less number.

## FARES BY DISTANCE.

### WITHIN A RADIUS OF FOUR MILES FROM CHARING CROSS.

Sixpence for any distance within, and not exceeding one mile.

For any distance exceeding one mile, at the rate of sixpence for every mile, and for any part of a mile not completed.

Where the fare now payable by law on hiring any hackney carriage standing on any stand shall not amount to one shilling, the driver shall be entitled to charge one shilling.

Above the number of two persons carried, sixpence extra for each person for the whole hiring.

Two children under the age of ten to be counted as one adult person.

One shilling for every mile, or part of a mile beyond four miles (radius) from Charing Cross, if carriage discharged beyond such four miles.

No driver shall demand or receive any sum by way of Back Fare, for the return of the carriage from the place at which discharged.

When the driver shall be required by the hirer to stop for fifteen minutes, or for any longer time, the driver may demand and receive a further sum (above the fare to which he shall be entitled, calculated according to distance) of sixpence for every fifteen minutes completed, that he shall have been so stopped.

## FARES BY TIME.

One hour, or any part of an hour, 2s.

For every fifteen minutes, or less, beyond one hour, 6d.

Each person above two, the whole hiring, 6d. extra.

No driver shall demand or receive any sum by way of Back Fare, for the return of the carriage from the place at which discharged.

If the driver is required to drive more than four miles in one hour, for every mile or part of a mile above four miles, 6d. extra.

Two children, under the age of ten, to be counted as one adult person.

## London Cab Fares and Regulations—*continued*.

### LUGGAGE.

A reasonable quantity of luggage is to be carried in or upon the carriage without any additional charge, except :—

When more than two persons are carried inside any hackney carriage, with more luggage than can be carried inside the carriage, a sum of 2d. for every package carried outside the carriage is to be paid.

### GENERAL REGULATIONS.

Hackney carriage standing in the street, unless actually hired, to be deemed plying for hire ; and the driver obliged to go with any person desirous of hiring such carriage ; should he refuse, the driver must produce evidence of having been actually hired at the time.

The driver is to drive at a reasonable and proper speed, not less than six miles an hour, unless in cases of unavoidable delay, or when required by the hirer to drive slower.

### OMNIBUSES.

The charge for Omnibus conveyance, in London, ranges from 2d. to 6d. per passenger, according to distance. By the last Street Traffic Regulation Omnibuses are now required to keep to their proper side of the street (the left-hand side), and they are not allowed to cross over to the opposite side either to set down or take up passengers.

STATISTICS OF CABS AND OMNIBUSES.—Total number of Cabs (in 1869)
Licensed for hire, in and about London* . . . . . 5,874
Total number of Omnibuses do. do. . . 1,050
Total Number of Cab Drivers . . . . . . . 7,910
Ditto Omnibus Drivers . . . . . . 1,427
Ditto Omnibus Conductors . . . . . . 1,561

\* *Of this number, 2439 work six days, and 3435 seven days.*

### COMMISSIONAIRES' TARIFF.

BY DISTANCE.—2d. half a mile or under ; 3d. one mile, and over half a mile.

BY TIME.—6d. per hour, or 2d. per quarter of an hour. When taken by time the Commissionaire is to do 2½ miles per hour, if walking. Should the Employer pay the fare of a Commissionaire by rail, boat, or omnibus, he may require him to execute his duty by the time tariff.

N.B.—The Commissionaires may charge 1d. per mile for every seven pounds exceeding one stone.

BY DAY of ten hours, 3s.; for four hours, 1s. 6d. Calling carriages, 2d. No return fare except when employed, or if sent more than three miles from post.

N.B.—In sending parcels, &c., Employers are requested to note the time of despatch on the outside, in order that the receiver may ascertain whether any delay has occurred. The usual rate of walking may be taken at 3½ miles per hour, or 5 per boat or omnibus.

THE LAW OF THE ROAD.—(Horses and Vehicle Traffic.) In this country the law of the road is that horses and carriages should respectively keep the left side of the road, and consequently in meeting should pass each other on the whip hand; and the Judges have so far confirmed it as to declare frequently at *nisi prius* that he who disregard this salutary rule is answerable in damages for all the consequences.

# Statistics of Railways in the United Kingdom.

*(Compiled for Bradshaw's Diary from the latest Board of Trade Returns.)*

| | |
|---|---|
| Total Capital authorised ... ... ... | £642,853,408 |
| Total Capital paid up (31st Dec., 1867) ... | £502,267,887 |
| Lines open for Traffic (at 31st Dec., 1867)... | 14,247 miles. |

### Number of Passengers conveyed:—

| | |
|---|---|
| First Class ... ... ... | £31,725,708 |
| Second Class ... ... ... | 77,700,297 |
| Third Class ... ... ... | 178,262,108 |

287,688,113 Passengers.

| | |
|---|---|
| General Merchandise conveyed ... | 46,474,037 Tons. |
| Minerals of all kinds conveyed ... | 98,633,791 Tons. |
| Live Stock conveyed ... ... ... ... | 15,724,058 Heads. |

### Number of Trains Run:—

| | |
|---|---|
| Passengers ... ... ... | 3,924,624 |
| Goods, Minerals, and Cattle ... | 2,403,866 |

6,328,490 Trains.

### Number of Miles run by Trains:—

| | |
|---|---|
| Passenger ... ... ... | 74,886,409 |
| Goods, Mineral, and Cattle ... | 73,656,418 |

148,542,827 Miles.

### Rolling Stock employed :—

| | |
|---|---|
| Locomotive Engines ... ... | 8,619 |
| Passenger Carriages ... ... | 19,773 |
| Other Passenger Vehicles ... | 7,581 |
| Goods, Mineral Wagons, &c. ... | 247,048 |

283,021

### Accidents to Passengers :—

| | |
|---|---|
| Killed from causes beyond their own control | 19, or 1 in every 15,000,000 carried. |
| Injured do. do. do. a large proportion being only trivial injuries | 689, or 1 in every 500,000 carried. |
| Killed through their own misconduct or want of caution .. .. .. .. .. | 17, or 1 in every 17,000,000 carried. |
| Injured from their own misconduct or want of caution .. .. .. .. .. | 8, or 1 in every 36,000,000 carried. |

*Land Occupied by Railways* —The land held by Railway Companies whose lines are open is 162,325 acres, or an average of about 12½ acres per lineal mile of Railway.

## Length of Railways Open Abroad :—

| | Miles open. | | Miles open. |
|---|---|---|---|
| Austria | 4,000 | Portugal | 600 |
| Belgium | 1,419 | Prussia | 5,764 |
| Canada | 2,495 | Russia | 2,056 |
| Chili | 336 | South Australia | 56 |
| France | 8,932 | Spain | 2,524 |
| Holland | 659 | Sweden | 532 |
| India | 3,943 | United States | 60,000 |
| Mexico | 300 | Victoria | 276 |
| Papal States | 84 | | |

# RAILWAYS IN THE UNITED KINGDOM.

*(Compiled for Bradshaw's Diary.)*

| NAME OF RAILWAY. | Miles open, 1869. | NAME OF RAILWAY, | Miles open, 1869. |
|---|---|---|---|
| Belfast and County Down ... | 44¼ | London Chatham and Dover... | 136¾ |
| Belfast and Northern Counties | 99¾ | London Chatham and Dover— | |
| Blyth and Tyne ... ... ... | 20 | Metropolitan Extension ... | 14 |
| Brecon and Merthyr ... ... | 59½ | London Chatham and Dover— | |
| Bristol and Exeter ... ... | 134¼ | Kent Coast Branch ... ... | 27 |
| | | London Tilbury and Southend | 42¼ |
| Caledonian ... ... ... ... | 668 | Londonderry and Coleraine ... | 36¼ |
| Cambrian ... ... ... ... | 178 | London and North Western ... | 1423¾ |
| Cork and Bandon ... ... ... | 20 | London and South Western ... | 521 |
| Cork and Limerick Direct ... | 25 | | |
| Cornwall ... ... ... ... | 65½ | Manchester and South Junction | 9¼ |
| | | Manchester Sheffield and | |
| Dublin and Belfast ... ... | 63 | Lincolnshire ... ... ... | 249 |
| Dublin and Drogheda ... ... | 75· | Maryport and Carlisle ... ... | 38 |
| Dublin and Meath ... ... | 35 | Metropolitan ... ... ... | 7½ |
| Dublin, Wicklow, and Wexford | 107 | Metropolitan District ... ... | 2¼ |
| | | Metropolitan and St. John's | |
| Furness Railway — Ulverston | | Wood ... ... ... ... | ... |
| and Lancaster ... ... ... | 93 | Midland ... ... ... ... | 770½ |
| | | Midland Great Western ... | 260¾ |
| Glasgow and South Western... | 249 | Monmouthshire ... ... ... | 44 |
| Great Eastern ... ... ... | 746 | | |
| Great Northern ... ... ... | 487 | North Eastern ... ... ... | 1258½ |
| Great North of Scotland ... | 256¾ | North London ... ... ... | 12 |
| Do. Morayshire ... | 18¼ | North Staffordshire Railway | |
| Great North and West of | | and Canal ... ... ... ... | 275 |
| Ireland ... ... ... ... | 91 | North British ... ... ... | 757½ |
| Great Southern and Western, | | | |
| Irish South Eastern, Killar- | | Pembroke and Tenby ... ... | 27 |
| ney Junction, Tralee, and | | | |
| Cork and Youghal ... ... | 419¾ | Rhymney ... ... ... ... | 22¾ |
| Great Western ... ... ... | 1387 | | |
| | | Somerset and Dorset ... ... | 66 |
| Highland ... ... ... ... | 245¾ | South Devon ... ... ... | 110½ |
| | | South Eastern ... ... ... | 346 |
| Irish North Western ... ... | 145 | Swansea Vale ... ... ... | 20 |
| Isle of Wight ... ... ... ... | 12 | | |
| | | Taff Vale ... ... ... ... | 63 |
| Kilkenny Junction ... ... ... | 28½ | | |
| | | Ulster ... ... ... ... ... | 105½ |
| Lancashire and Yorkshire ... | 411½ | | |
| Limerick and Ennis ... ... | 24¾ | Waterford and Kilkenny ... | 31 |
| Limerick and Foynes ... ... | 26¼ | Waterford and Limerick ... | 77 |
| Llanelly ... ... ... ... | 41¼ | Whitehaven Cleator and | |
| Lynvi and Ogmore ... ... | 30¼ | Egremont ... ... ... | 10 |
| London Brighton and South | | Wrexham Mold and Connah's | |
| Coast ... ... ... ... ... | 365¼ | Quay ... ... ... ... ... | 14 |

# DATES OF OPENING SOME OF THE RAILWAYS IN THE UNITED KINGDOM.

*(Compiled for Bradshaw's Diary.)*

| LENGTH OF RAILWAY. | DATE OF OPENING. |
|---|---|
| Stockton to Darlington | 27th September, 1825. |
| Canterbury to Whitstable | May, 1830. |
| Manchester to Liverpool | 15th September, 1830. |
| Edinburgh to Dalkeith | June, 1831. |
| Leeds to Selby | 24th September, 1834. |
| Dublin to Kingstown | 17th December, 1834. |
| London to Greenwich | 1836. |
| Paddington to Hanwell | 3rd May, 1837. |
| Birmingham to Liverpool | 4th July, 1837. |
| London to Birmingham | 17th September, 1838. |
| Liverpool to Preston | 31st October, 1838. |
| Manchester to Leeds | 31st October, 1838. |
| Sheffield to Rotherham | October, 1838. |
| Derby to Nottingham | 30th May, 1839. |
| London to Croydon | 1st June, 1839. |
| London to Basingstoke | 10th June, 1839. |
| London to Romford | 18th June, 1839. |
| Newcastle to Carlisle | 18th June, 1839. |
| Newcastle to North Shields | 18th June, 1839. |
| Birmingham to Derby | 12th August, 1839. |
| London to Reading | 30th March, 1840. |
| Dundee and Arbroath | 8th April, 1840. |
| London to Southampton | 11th May, 1840. |
| Derby to Sheffield | 11th May, 1840. |
| York to Normanton | 30th June, 1840. |
| Derby to Leeds | July, 1840. |
| Derby to Rugby | July, 1840. |
| London to Bristol | 31st August, 1840. |
| Glasgow to Ayr | 19th September, 1840. |
| Chester to Birkenhead | 22nd September, 1840. |
| Chester to Crewe | 1st October, 1840. |
| Birmingham to Gloucester | 17th December, 1840. |
| Greenock Railway | 31st May, 1841. |
| Fenchurch Street to Blackwall | 2nd August, 1841. |
| London to Brighton | 21st September, 1841. |
| Edinburgh to Glasgow | 8th February, 1842. |
| London to Ashford (Kent) | 1st December, 1842. |
| London to Folkestone | 28th June, 1843. |
| London to Dover | 7th February, 1844. |
| Newcastle to Darlington | 1844. |
| Bristol to Exeter | 1st May, 1844. |
| Dublin and Drogheda | 26th May, 1844. |
| London to Oxford | 12th June, 1844. |
| Gravesend to Rochester | 10th February, 1845. |
| Norwich to Yarmouth | 1st May, 1845. |
| Swindon to Cheltenham | 12th May, 1845. |

# Dates of Opening some of the Railways in the United Kingdom.—*Continued.*

*(Compiled for Bradshaw's Diary.)*

| Length of Railway. | Date of Opening. |
| --- | --- |
| Northampton to Peterborough | 2nd June, 1845. |
| York to Scarborough | 7th July, 1845. |
| Bristol to Gloucester | July, 1845. |
| London to Tunbridge Wells | September, 1845. |
| Manchester to Sheffield | 22nd December, 1845. |
| London to Ramsgate and Margate | 6th February, 1846. |
| Colchester to Ipswich | 15th June, 1846. |
| Leeds to Bradford | 1st July, 1846. |
| London to Richmond | 27th July, 1846 |
| Nottingham to Lincoln | 3rd August, 1846. |
| Shrewsbury to Chester | 4th November, 1846. |
| Brighton to Hastings | 5th November, 1846. |
| Croydon to Epsom | 17th May, 1847. |
| Dundee and Perth | 22nd May, 1847. |
| Brighton to Portsmouth | 14th June, 1847. |
| Kendal to Windermere | 21st August, 1847. |
| Trent Valley | 1st December, 1847. |
| Caledonian Railway | 1848. |
| London to Rochester | 30th July, 1849. |
| London to Peterborough | August, 1850. |
| Tunbridge Wells to Hastings | 1st February, 1852. |
| Dublin to Belfast | June, 1852. |
| King's Cross Station | October, 1852. |
| London Bridge to Crystal Palace | 10th June, 1854. |
| Aberdeen to Inverness | 18th August, 1858. |
| Victoria (L. B. & S. C. R.) Station | 2nd October, 1860. |
| Canterbury to Dover | 1st November, 1861. |
| Metropolitan Railway | 10th January, 1863. |
| First Railway Train over Charing Cross Rlwy. Bdg. | 2nd December, 1863. |
| Charing Cross and London Bridge | 11th January, 1864. |
| Beckenham to Croydon | 4th April, 1864. |
| Ryde to Shanklin | 23rd August, 1864. |
| First Railway Train over Blackfriars Bridge | 6th October, 1864. |
| New Cross to Chislehurst | 1st July, 1865. |
| Horsham to Guildford | 2nd October, 1865. |
| Alton to Winchester | 2nd October, 1865. |
| Weymouth to Portland | 16th October, 1865. |
| Broad Street Station | 1st November, 1865. |
| Moorgate Street Station | 23rd December, 1865. |
| Cannon Street Station | 1st September, 1866. |
| Chislehurst to Sevenoaks | 2nd March, 1868. |
| Sutherland Railway | 13th April, 1868. |
| Baker Street to Swiss Cottage | 13th April, 1868. |
| Sevenoaks to Tunbridge | 1st May, 1868 |
| St. Pancras (Midland) Station | 1st October, 1868. |
| South Kensington to Westminster Bridge | 24th December, 1868. |

# CHRONOLOGICAL TABLE OF ROYAL VISITS, &c.

*(Compiled for Bradshaw's Diary).*

| | |
|---|---|
| February 6, 1840. | Prince Albert arrived at Dover. |
| February 8, 1840. | Do.          do.    in London. |
| January 14, 1842. | King Prussia, visit to England. |
| August, 1842. | Queen and Prince Albert first visit to Scotland. |
| September, 1843. | Queen and Prince Albert to France and Belgium. |
| June, 1844. | Emperor of Russia, visit to England. |
| October, 1844. | Louis Phillippe, visit to England. |
| August, 1845. | Queen and Prince Albert to Germany. |
| June, 1846. | Grand Duke Constantine, visit to England. |
| August, 1849. | Queen and Prince Albert to Ireland. |
| May, 1850. | Nepaulese Embassy to England. |
| August, 1850. | Queen and Prince Albert to Belgium. |
| August, 1850. | Ditto          ditto        to Scotland. |
| October, 1851. | Ditto          ditto        to Manchester and Liverpool. |
| August, 1852. | Ditto          ditto        to Belgium. |
| October, 1852. | King Belgium and Son, visit to England. |
| August, 1853. | Queen and Prince Albert to Ireland. |
| June, 1854. | King of Portugal, visit to England. |
| September, 1854. | Prince Albert to Bolougne. |
| April, 1855. | Emperor and Empress of French, visit to England. |
| August, 1855. | Queen and Prince Albert to France. |
| November, 1855. | King Sardinia, visit to England. |
| July, 1856. | Queen of Oude, visit to England. |
| April, 1857. | Grand Duke Constantine to England. |
| June, 1857. | Queen and Prince Albert to Manchester. |
| August, 1857. | Emperor and Empress French, visit to Osborne. |
| October, 1857. | Siamese Embassy to England. |
| January, 1858. | Prince Frederick William Prussia, visit to England. |
| June, 1858. | Queen and Prince Albert to Birmingham. |
| August, 1858. | Ditto          ditto        to Cherbourg and Prussia. |
| August, 1858. | Ditto          ditto        to Leeds. |
| 1859. | Prince Wales, Tour of the Continent. |
| June, 1860. | King Belgium and Son, visit to England. |
| July, 1860. | Prince Wales to Canada and United States. |
| September, 1860. | Queen and Prince Albert to Prussia. |
| November, 1860. | Empress French, visit to England and Scotland. |
| November, 1860. | Empress Austria, visit to Madeira. |
| August, 1861. | King Sweden and Prince Oscar, visit to England. |
| August, 1861. | Prince Wales to Ireland. |
| May, 1862. | Viceroy Egypt, visit to England. |
| May, 1862. | Japanese Embassy to England. |
| June, 1862. | Prince Louis of Hesse arrived in England. |
| November, 1862. | Princess Alexandra, visit to Osborne and Windsor. |
| November, 1862. | Prince of Wales to Germany and the East. |
| March, 1863. | Princess Alexandra arrived in London. |
| April, 1864. | Garibaldi, visit to England. |
| August, 1865. | Abd el Kader, visit to England. |
| December, 1865. | King Portugal, visit to England. |
| 1866. | King and Queen Belgium, visit to England. |
| August, 1866. | Prince and Princess Wales to York. |
| March, 1867. | King of Denmark, visit to England. |
| April, 1867. | Prince of Wales to Paris. |
| July, 1867. | Viceroy of Egypt, visit to England. |
| July, 1867. | The Sultan of Turkey, visit to England. |
| August, 1867. | Queen visited Kelso, Melrose, &c. |
| August, 1867. | Prince and Princess of Wales to the Continent. |
| October, 1867. | Chinese Embassy to England. |
| December, 1867. | Brother Tycoon Japan, visit to England. |
| December, 1867. | Duke of Edinburgh, visit to Australian Colonies. |
| April, 1868. | Prince Wales to Ireland. |
| August, 1868. | Queen to France and Switzerland. |
| November, 1868. | Prince and Princess of Wales to Denmark, the Continent, Egypt, &c. |
| March, 1869. | Chinese Embassy to England. |
| June, 1869. | Viceroy of Egypt, visit to England. |

# GENERAL INFORMATION, SUGGESTIONS, &c., FOR RAILWAY TRAVELLERS.

(Compiled for Bradshaw's Diary and applicable to all Railways in the United Kingdom.)

CLOCK TIME.—The time kept at all Railway Stations in England, Wales, and Scotland is Greenwich time. Time at Dublin, and on Irish Railways, is about 20 minutes after Greenwich time. The Guards of the various Companies' Trains also carry this time. For time at other parts of the world, as compared with Greenwich time, see page 36.

TIME OF TRAINS, &c.—For the correct time of departure of Trains, the respective Railway Companies' Official Time-books, or "Bradshaw's" and other authorized Guides, should be consulted. Railway Time Service, as a general rule, is revised on the first of each month; consequently it is necessary that careful reference or inquiry should be made on the first day or two of the month, as to the time of any particular Train.

BOOKING OFFICE, &c.—Passengers should be at the Station of departure at least five minutes before the advertised time. They should refer to the Table of Fares usually exhibited in each Booking Office, and have the amount of their fare ready for the Booking Clerk, so as to save time at the Booking Counter. The Railway Ticket should always be kept ready for production on the journey, so as to avoid delay in searching for it. Passengers should accustom themselves to keeping their Ticket in one particular pocket or place; and (in case of loss.) the No. on the Ticket should be noted. This is especially suggested when Passengers are travelling any considerable distance. Change should always be examined before the Passenger leaves the Counter, as mistakes are not afterwards recognised by the Company.

CHILDREN under 3 years of age, free; above 3 and under 12, half-price (with very few exceptions, this is the arrangement on all Lines). Care should be taken that Children do not have their fingers about the doorway when the Carriage doors are open or being closed, and that they do not lean or push against the doors on the journey in case of the door being left unfastened.

LUGGAGE.—Passengers with large quantities of Luggage should be at the Station at least 15 minutes before the advertised time of departure, so that the Luggage may be properly labelled, loaded, &c. All old labels should be obliterated, or washed off Luggage to prevent mistakes. Passengers should always see their Luggage labelled, and put into the van. A few loose, small articles of Luggage may be taken in the carriages with the Passengers if desired, but they should be put either under the seat or in the netting of the carriage so as not to occupy a seat. In the event of Luggage being missing, the fact should at once be made known to the Guard or Station Master. The average usual weight of Personal Luggage allowed each Passenger is about 120 lbs. first class, 100 lbs. second class, and 56 lbs. third class.

# General Information, Suggestions, &c., for Railway Travellers—*continued*.

**WAITING ROOMS.**—As a general rule there is a female attendant at every principal Railway Station Ladies' Room. A glass of cold water is generally to be obtained in the Ladies' Rooms.

**A CLOAK-ROOM** is provided at every Station, where all Articles left for the convenience of the Passenger should be deposited, the Company not being responsible for articles left on any other part of the Station, or in the care of any of their officers or servants, except the officers in charge at the Cloak-room.

**OUTSIDE PORTERS, &c.**—Outside Porters or Commissionaires for hire, at a moderate fixed tariff, are now attached to all principal Railway Stations, for carrying Luggage, conveying Messages, &c.

**INQUIRIES.**—Passengers should make their inquiries at the Station before the time of booking, and as much as possible avoid asking the Booking Clerk questions at the time of booking.

**REFRESHMENT ROOMS** are provided at all principal Railway Stations, and the time allowed is generally ruled by the punctuality of the train, as for instance, if the train be late, the usual stopping time is expected to be curtailed.

**TELEGRAPH MESSAGES.**—Nearly all principal Stations are now Telegraph Depôts, and in case of urgency a Message Form may (through the Guard of the Train) be obtained at one Station, filled up during the progress of the train, and given in for transmission at the next Station the train stops at.

**TO PREVENT ACCIDENTS.**—Passengers should not lean upon or open the carriage-door, or step from or into any of the carriages when the train is in motion. There is also risk in leave-taking by shaking hands when the train is in motion. Passengers should be very careful to see that the door of their carriage is secured before the train starts, that no part of their clothing or dress is caught in the door, and that they do not open the door to alight without first looking to see that it is the proper platform side of the train to do so. Passengers should also take care not to have their hand or fingers caught when a door is closed.

**PASSENGERS TRAVELLING LONG DISTANCES** should remember the number of their carriage so as to find it again readily when alighting at the Station on the journey for refreshments, &c., and it is also well to take a note of it in case of anything being left behind. Long-journey Passengers should also select the seats the farthest from the near or Station side door, so as not to be disturbed by the short-journey passengers getting in and out.

**FEET WARMERS.**—These are supplied to first-class Passengers during cold weather for journeys of sufficient length to require them. Some of the Railway Companies make a small charge for Feet Warmers.

**POST OFFICE LETTER BOXES AT RAILWAY STATIONS.**—Nearly all principal Stations are now provided with Post Office Letter Boxes for the convenience of Passengers who may require to post a letter during a journey.

# TABLE OF GEOGRAPHICAL EPOCHS, &c.

*(Compiled for Bradshaw's Diary.)*

| | |
|---|---|
| First Expedition of Columbus | Aug. 3, 1492, to March 15, 1493 |
| Second Expedition of Columbus | Sept. 25, 1493, to June 8, 1496 |
| Third Expedition of Columbus | May 30, 1498, to Nov. 20, 1500 |
| Fourth Expedition of Columbus | May 9, 1501, to Oct., 1504 |
| Voyage of John Cabot | Commenced in May, 1494 |
| Voyage of his Son, Sebastian Cabot | Commenced in May, 1497 |
| Voyage of Vasco de Gama | July 8, 1497, to Sept. 20, 1499 |
| Voyage of Magellan | August 10, 1519; killed in 1521 |
| Voyage of Sir Francis Drake | Dec. 13, 1577, to Sept. 26, 1580 |
| Voyage of Commodore Anson | Sept. 18, 1740, to June 15, 1744 |
| First Voyage of Captain James Cook | August 26, 1768, to July 12, 1771 |
| Second Voyage of Captain James Cook | July 13, 1772, to July 30, 1775 |
| Voyage of Cook, Clerke, and Gore | July 12, 1776, to Aug. 22, 1780 |
| Voyage of Capt. Jean F. G. de la Perouse | August 1, 1785 ; lost in 1788 |
| Voyage of Capt. George Vancouver | April 1, 1791, to Nov. 22, 1795 |
| United States Expedition, Capt. Wilkes | Aug. 18, 1838, to June 10, 1842 |
| Sir John Franklin (his last Expedition) | May 23, 1845 |
| Voyage of Arctic Expedition sailed | July 1, 1857 |

| | |
|---|---|
| Cuba discovered | October 7, 1492 |
| America discovered | October 12, 1492 |
| Bahamas discovered | 1492 |
| Island of Jamaica discovered | March 4, 1494 |
| Canada and Nova Scotia discovered | 1497 |
| Natal discovered | 1497 |
| St. Vincent and Trinidad discovered | 1498 |
| Brazil discovered | April 24, 1500 |
| Island of St. Helena discovered | July 31, 1502 |
| Honduras discovered | 1502 |
| Madagascar discovered | August 10, 1506 |
| Mauritius discovered | 1507 |
| Ascension Island discovered | 1508 |
| South Sea discovered | September 25, 1513 |
| Pacific Ocean discovered | November 27, 1519 |
| Borneo discovered | 1521 |
| Bermudas discovered | 1527 |
| Virginia discovered | 1584 |
| First Settlement of the English in India | 1591 |
| Barbadoes discovered | 1600 |
| First European Settlement in America | 1603 |
| New South Wales discovered | March 6, 1606 |
| New Zealand discovered | 1642 |
| Tasmania discovered | 1642 |
| Queensland discovered | 1770 |
| Sandwich Islands discovered | 1778 |
| Sydney, Australia founded | January 26, 1788 |
| Gold discovered in California | September 10, 1847 |
| Gold discovered in Australia | April 12, 1851 |
| Source of the Nile discovered | February 23, 1863 |

# CHRONOLOGICAL LANDMARKS.

*(From Whitaker's Almanack.)*

| Years since. | B.C. | | Years since. | A.D. | | Years since. | A.D. |
|---|---|---|---|---|---|---|---|
| 5873 | The Creation of the world | 4004 | 1873 | Birth of our Lord, 4 years bef. Ch. era | 4 | 654 | King John granted Magna Charta ...... 1215 |
| 4217 | The Deluge | 2348 | 1840 | The Crucifixion of our Lord | 29 | 604 | First Representative Parliament ...... 1265 |
| 3790 | The Call of Abraham | 1921 | 1826 | Invasion of Britain by Aulus Plautius | 43 | 587 | Wales was conquered by Edward I. ... 1282 |
| 3731 | Joseph was sold into Egypt | 1862 | 1808 | Revolt of the Britons under Boadicea | 61 | 564 | Wallace was captured and executed ... 1305 |
| 3494 | The Exodus under Moses | 1625 | 1799 | Jerusalem was destroyed | 70 | 563 | Robert Bruce King of Scotland ...... 1306 |
| 3149 | Canaan divided among the tribes | 1580 | 1749 | The Emperor Hadrian visited Britain | 120 | 542 | Edward II. deposed and murdered ...... 1327 |
| 3052 | The Fall of Troy | 1183 | 1556 | Constantine embraced Christianity | 313 | 523 | Battle of Crécy: the French defeated... 1346 |
| 2851 | Era of Cheops; Great Pyramid | 1082 | 1539 | Constantinople made the capital | 330 | 523 | Battle of Nevill's Cross ...... 1346 |
| 2818 | David became King of Israel | 1049 | 1460 | Rome sacked by Alaric | 409 | 522 | Calais captured by Edward III. ...... 1347 |
| 2382 | The Temple of Jerusalem founded | 1013 | 1451 | The Romans finally quitted Britain | 418 | 513 | The French were defeated at Poictiers 1356 |
| 2815 | Division of Solomon's Kingdom | 976 | 1420 | Vortigern called in the aid of Saxons | 449 | 488 | Wat Tyler's Rebellion ...... 1381 |
| 2831 | Probable era of Homer (from 915 to | 962 | 1415 | Saxon kingdom founded in Kent | 454 | 481 | Battle of Otterburn (or Chevy Chase)... 1388 |
| 2741 | Carthage was founded | 878 | 1042 | Egbert, first king of all England | 827 | 470 | Richard II. was deposed ...... 1399 |
| 2639 | The Olympic era commenced | 776 | 993 | Alfred the Great succeeded to the Crown | 871 | 454 | The Battle of Agincourt ...... 1415 |
| 2616 | Foundation of Rome; era A. U. C. | 753 | 957 | The Norsemen conquered Neustria | 912 | 440 | Joan of Arc raised the Siege of Orleans 1429 |
| 2474 | The Babylonian Captivity commenced. | 605 | 890 | King Edward the Martyr murdered | 979 | 414 | The wars of the Roses commenced ...... 1455 |
| 2456 | Jerusalem taken by Nebuchadnezzar | 587 | 852 | Canute of Denmark king of England | 1017 | 408 | The House of York came to the Throne 1461 |
| 2398 | Death of Cyrus | 529 | 803 | The Battle of Hastings | 1066 | 393 | Warwick was killed at Barnet ...... 1471 |
| 2373 | Expulsion of the Tarquins | 509 | 783 | The Domesday survey completed | 1086 | 384 | Richard III. killed at Bosworth ...... 1485 |
| 2349 | Xerxes was defeated at Thermopylæ | 480 | 773 | The Crusades commenced | 1096 | 356 | Battle of Flodden; Scots defeated ...... 1513 |
| 1924 | Cæsar's invasion of Britain | 55 | 769 | William Rufus was killed | 1100 | 330 | Monasteries were dissolved ...... 1529 |
| 1913 | The murder of Cæsar | 44 | 689 | The Murder of Thomas à Becket | 1170 | 314 | The Marian persecution began ...... 1555 |
| 1896 | Octavius became Emperor | 27 | 679 | Richard I. went to the Crusades | 1190 | 313 | Archbishop Cranmer burnt ...... 1556 |

## Chronological Landmarks.—*Continued.*

| Years since. | | A.D. |
|---|---|---|
| 311 | Calais was taken from the English | 1558 |
| 311 | Accession of Queen Elizabeth | 1558 |
| 297 | The St. Bartholomew Massacre | 1572 |
| 282 | Mary Queen of Scots was beheaded | 1587 |
| 281 | The Spanish Armada was defeated | 1588 |
| 264 | The Gunpowder Plot | 1605 |
| 229 | The Long Parliament assembled | 1640 |
| 227 | The Battle of Edgehill | 1642 |
| 224 | Battle of Naseby; the king defeated | 1645 |
| 220 | Charles I. was beheaded, 30th January | 1649 |
| 216 | Oliver Cromwell Lord Protector | 1653 |
| 209 | The Monarchy was restored | 1660 |
| 184 | Duke of Monmouth's rebellion | 1685 |
| 180 | Parliament elected William and Mary | 1689 |
| 179 | The Battle of the Boyne | 1690 |
| 177 | The Glencoe Massacre | 1692 |
| 165 | The Battle of Blenheim | 1704 |
| 165 | Gibraltar was taken by the English | 1704 |
| 156 | The Treaty of Utrecht | 1713 |
| 155 | The Accession of the House of Hanover | 1714 |
| 149 | The South Sea Bubble | 1720 |
| 126 | The Battle of Dettingen | 1743 |
| 124 | The Battle of Fontenoy | 1745 |
| 124 | The Scotch Rebellion | 1745 |
| 94 | Battle of Lexington, first American | 1775 |
| 87 | Independence of the United States | 1782 |
| 76 | Louis XVI. of France was executed | 1793 |

| Years since. | | A.D. |
|---|---|---|
| 72 | The Mutiny at the Nore | 1797 |
| 71 | The Irish Rebellion | 1798 |
| 71 | The Battle of the Nile | 1798 |
| 68 | The Union of Great Britain and Ireland | 1801 |
| 68 | The British Expedition to Egypt | 1801 |
| 67 | The Treaty of Amiens | 1802 |
| 66 | The war with France resumed | 1803 |
| 64 | Bonaparte Emperor of the French | 1805 |
| 64 | Battle of Trafalgar; death of Nelson | 1805 |
| 60 | The Battle of Corunna | 1809 |
| 57 | The French expedition to Russia | 1812 |
| 55 | The Restoration of the Bourbons | 1814 |
| 54 | The Battle of Waterloo; 18th June | 1815 |
| 53 | The Bombardment of Algiers | 1816 |
| 49 | The Trial of Queen Caroline | 1820 |
| 47 | The Greek Revolution broke out | 1822 |
| 45 | The first Burmese war commenced | 1824 |
| 43 | The Insurrection of the Janissaries | 1826 |
| 42 | The Battle of Navarino | 1827 |
| 39 | Revolution in France; Charles X. exp. | 1830 |
| 37 | The first Reform Act passed, 7th June | 1832 |
| 36 | The Carlist war in Spain | 1833 |
| 35 | English Poor Law Amendment Act | 1834 |
| 35 | The Houses of Parliament were burnt | 1834 |
| 32 | Accession of Queen Victoria, 20th June | 1837 |
| 31 | The Rebellion in Canada | 1838 |
| 30 | The War with China | 1839 |

| Years since. | | A.D. |
|---|---|---|
| 30 | The Affghan war commenced | 1839 |
| 30 | The Chartist riots at Newport | 1839 |
| 29 | Marriage of Queen Victoria | 1840 |
| 28 | Birth of the Prince of Wales, 9th Nov. | 1841 |
| 27 | The Imposition of the Income Tax | 1842 |
| 26 | Scinde was conquered | 1843 |
| 25 | The Civil War in Switzerland | 1844 |
| 24 | Sir John Franklin sailed | 1845 |
| 24 | The Sikhs were defeated at Moodkee | 1845 |
| 23 | Repeal of the Corn Laws, 26th June | 1846 |
| 22 | War between the U. S. and Mexico | 1847 |
| 21 | Chartist Assemblage, 10th April | 1848 |
| 21 | French Revolution, Louis Philippe exp. | 1848 |
| 18 | International Exhibition in London | 1851 |
| 17 | Louis Napoleon Emperor of French | 1852 |
| 15 | The Battle of Inkerman | 1854 |
| 14 | The Capture of Sebastopol | 1855 |
| 12 | The Indian Mutiny broke out | 1857 |
| 8 | The Death of the Prince Consort | 1861 |
| 7 | The Second International Exhibition | 1862 |
| 5 | War between Germany and Denmark | 1864 |
| 4 | The Death of Lord Palmerston | 1865 |
| 3 | The Seven Weeks' War | 1866 |
| 3 | Fenian outrages at Manchester, &c | 1867 |
| 2 | The New Reform Act passed | 1867 |
| 1 | Terrible earthquake in Peru | 1868 |

LONDON:
BRADSHAW & BLACKLOCK, PRINTERS, ALLEN STREET,
GOSWELL STREET, E.C.

4 SE69

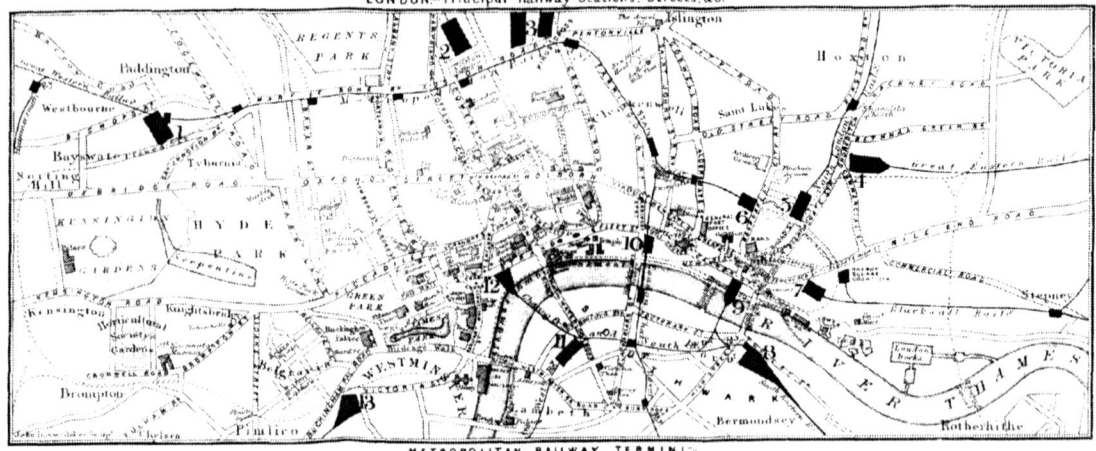

LONDON.—Principal Railway Stations, Streets, &c.

METROPOLITAN RAILWAY TERMINI:

Nº 1. *Paddington* . . . . . . *Great Western & Metropolitan*
2. *Euston Sqʳᵉ* . . . . . . *London & North Western*
3. *Kings Cross* . . . . . . *Great Northern & Metropolitan*
3. *Kings Cross* . . . . . . (*Midland*)

Nº 4. *Bishopsgate* . . . . . . *Great Eastern*
5. *Broad Street Gᵗᵉ* . . . . *North London*
6. *Moorgate Street* . . . . . *Metropolitan*
7. *Fenchurch Sᵗ* . . . . . . *Blackwall London & Tilbury*

Nº 8. *London Bridge* . . . . *South Eastern*
8. *Dᵒ* . . . . *Dᵒ* . . . . *London Brighton & Sᵗʰ Coast*
9. *Cannon Street* . . . . . . *South Eastern*
10. *Ludgate Hill* . . . . . . *London Chatham & Dover*

Nº 11. *Waterloo Road* . . . . *London & South Western*
12. *Charring Cross* . . . . . *South Eastern*
13. *Victoria (Pimlico)* . . . *London Brighton & Sᵗʰ Coast*
13. *Dᵒ* . . . . *Dᵒ* . . . . *London Chatham & Dover*

# RAILWAY ROUTES FROM LONDON.

## GREAT WESTERN RAILWAY.
PADDINGTON STATION.—No. 1.

**ROUTE** to Windsor, Reading, Oxford, Leamington, Warwick, Stratford-on-Avon, Birmingham, Wolverhampton, Shrewsbury, Chester, Birkenhead, Manchester, Liverpool and North Wales; also to Bath, Bristol, Bridgwater, Taunton, Exeter, Weymouth, Gloucester, Cheltenham, Hereford, Plymouth, Falmouth, Cornwall, Cardiff, Swansea; and the South of Ireland, *via* Milford and Waterford, &c.

## LONDON AND NORTH WESTERN RAILWAY.
EUSTON SQUARE STATION.—No. 2.

**ROUTE** to Watford, Aylesbury, Bedford, Northampton, Rugby, Coventry, Nuneaton, Birmingham, Lichfield, Tamworth, Stafford, Walsall, Wolverhampton, Crewe, Chester, Birkenhead, Manchester, Liverpool, Bangor and North Wales, Holyhead, Dublin, &c.; also to Huddersfield, Leeds, Preston, Fleetwood, Lancaster, Windermere, the English Lakes, Carlisle, Edinburgh, Glasgow, &c.

## GREAT NORTHERN RAILWAY.
KING'S CROSS.—No. 3.

**ROUTE** to St. Albans, Hertford, Cambridge, Huntingdon, Peterborough, Stamford, Boston, Lincoln, Grimsby, Grantham, Nottingham, Sheffield, Huddersfield, Barnsley, Manchester, Liverpool, Bury, Bolton, Doncaster, Wakefield, Leeds, Bradford, Halifax, Harrogate, Ripon, Hull, York, Scarboro', Durham, Newcastle-on-Tyne, Berwick-on-Tweed, Edinburgh, Glasgow, &c.

## MIDLAND RAILWAY.
KING'S CROSS.—No. 3.

**ROUTE** to Bedford, Northampton, Leicester, Melton Mowbray, Loughborough, Nottingham, Derby, Burton-on-Trent, North Staffordshire District; and to Matlock, Buxton, Sheffield, Wakefield, Leeds, Bradford, Lancaster, Westmoreland and the English Lakes; the North of Ireland, *via* Fleetwood; and, *via* Normanton and North-East Coast, to York, Newcastle, Edinburgh, Glasgow, &c.

## NORTH LONDON, METROPOLITAN, and BLACKWALL RAILWAYS. Nos. 5, 6, and 7.

**ROUTE**s to Metropolitan and Suburban Districts, as shown on the plan, &c.

## LONDON, BRIGHTON, AND SOUTH COAST RAILWAY.
LONDON BRIDGE AND VICTORIA. Nos. 8 & 13.

**ROUTE** to Crystal Palace, Croydon, Epsom, Leatherhead, East Grinstead, Horsham, Petworth, Midhurst, Portsmouth, Isle of Wight, Chichester, Bognor, Arundel, Littlehampton, Worthing, Shoreham, Brighton, Lewes, Uckfield, Seaford, Eastbourne, Hailsham, Hastings; and *via* Newhaven and Dieppe, to the Channel Islands, Paris, and the Continent, &c.

## LONDON, CHATHAM, AND DOVER.
LUDGATE HILL AND VICTORIA.—No. 10 & 13.

**ROUTE** to Crystal Palace, Bromley, Seven Oaks, Chatham, Rochester, Sittingbourne, Sheerness, Faversham, Whitstable, Herne Bay, Ramsgate, Broadstairs, Margate, Canterbury, Dover, Calais, Ostend, Paris, Belgium, Germany, Holland, Switzerland, the Rhine, Overland Route to India, *via* Marseilles, &c.

## GREAT EASTERN.
BISHOPSGATE STATION.—No. 4.

**ROUTE** to Brentford, Chelmsford, Colchester, Ipswich, Harwich, Norwich, Lowestoft, Yarmouth, Lynn, Hunstanton, Wisbeach, Peterborough, Cambridge, Ely, Newmarket, &c.; *via* Harwich, Antwerp and Rotterdam, to Belgium, Holland, Germany, the Rhine and Switzerland; also to Prussia, Sweden, Denmark, and the North of Europe, &c.

## SOUTH EASTERN.
CHARING CROSS, CANNON STREET, AND LONDON BRIDGE. Nos. 8, 9, 12.

**ROUTE** to Croydon, Greenwich, Woolwich, Dartford, Gravesend, Chatham, Reigate, Dorking, Guildford, Aldershot Camp, Reading, Rye, Wells St. Leonards, Hastings, Canterbury, Whitstable, Ramsgate, Margate, Deal, Rye, Maidstone, Sevenoaks, Hythe, Folkestone, Dover, Boulogne, Calais, Ostend, Paris, Belgium, Germany, Switzerland; Overland Route to India, *via* Marseilles, &c.

## LONDON AND SOUTH WESTERN RAILWAY.
WATERLOO STATION.—No. 11.

**ROUTE** to Hampton Court, Kingston, Richmond, Kew, Hounslow, Windsor, Epsom, Guildford, Petersfield, Egham, Ascot, Reading, Winchester, Portsmouth, Gosport, Southampton, Isle of Wight, the Channel Islands, also to Salisbury, Yeovil, Weymouth, Lymington, Poole, Exeter, Exmouth, Barnstaple, Bideford, North Devon; and *via* Southampton and Havre, to Paris and the Continent, &c.

ROUTES TO PARIS     PARIS: PRINCIPAL RAILWAY STATIONS: STREETS &c.

## RAILWAY STATIONS IN PARIS.

Nº 1 *Rue St Lazare & Rue d'Amsterdam* (*Western of France Rail*)    Nº 4 *Place de la Bastille* .......... *Eastern of France Rail*    Nº 7 *Barrière d'Enter* .......... *Scaux & D'Orsay Rail*
Nº 2 *Place Roubaix Rue de Dunkerque* (*Northern of France Rail*)    Nº 5 *Boulevart Marais* .......... *Lyons, Mediterranean Rail*    Nº 8 *Boulevart de Mont Parnasse* .......... *Western of France Rail*
Nº 3 *Place de Strasbourg* .......... *Eastern of France Rail*    Nº 6 *Boulevart de l'Hopital* .......... *Orleans Rail*

# RAILWAY ROUTES FROM PARIS.

**NORTHERN OF FRANCE RAILWAY.**
(CHEMIN DE FER DU NORD.)

*Place Roubaix, Rue Dunkerque.—No. 2.*

**ROUTE** to St. Denis, Chantilly, Senlis, Creil, Ermont, Beauvais, Soissons, Reims, Rethel, Charleville, Givet, Douai, Dunkirk, Valenciennes, Arras, Lille, Mouscron, Amiens, Abbeville, Clermont, Nogelles, St. Valery, St. Omer, Boulogne, Calais, Enghien, Pontoise, Compiègne, Noyon, Forgnier, St. Quentin, Bruges, Maubeuge, Mons, Brussels, Ghent, Erquelines, Charleroi, Namur, Liège, Spa, Verviers, Aix-la-Chapelle, Cologne, Bonn, Coblentz, Ems, Wiesbaden, Homburg, Mayence, Francfort, Berlin, Leipsic, Dresden, Warsaw, St. Petersburg, &c.; also, to London, *via* Boulogne and Folkestone, and Calais and Dover, (the Tidal and Mail Express Routes), &c.

**WESTERN OF FRANCE RAILWAY.**
(CHEMIN DE FER DE L'OUEST.)

*Rue St. Lazare, and Rue d'Amsterdam.—No. 1.*

**ROUTE** to Saint Cloud, Sevres, Versailles, St. Germain, Mantes, Vernon, Lisieux, Trouville, Caen, Bayeux, St. Lo, Honfleur, Cherbourg, &c.; Tourville, Clever, Rouen, Pecamp, Harfleur, Havre, Dieppe, &c.; also, to London, *via* Dieppe and Newhaven, or Havre and Southampton, &c.

(CHEMIN DE FER DE L'OUEST.)

*Boulevard du Mont Parnasse.—No. 8.*

**ROUTE** to Bologne, Sevres, Versailles (left bank of Seine), Rambouillet, Chartres, Le Mans, Laval-Vitre, Rennes, St. Brieuc, Guingamp, Morlaix, Brest, &c.; Angers, Laval, St. Malo, Lorient, Mayenne, Dreux, Alençon, &c.

(CHEMIN DE FER D'ORLEANS ET DU MIDI.)

*Barrière d'Enter.—No. 7.*

**ROUTE** to Bourg-la-Reine, Fontenay, Sceaux, Orsay, &c.

**EASTERN OF FRANCE RAILWAY.**
(CHEMIN DE FER DE L'EST.) *Place de Strasbourg.—No. 3.*

**ROUTE** to Meaux, Epernay, Reims, Charleville, Chalons-s-Marne, Nancy, Metz, Luxembourg, Treves, Namur, Liège, Strasbourg, Girat, Troyes, Chaumont, Baden Baden, Carlsruhe, Heidelberg, Mannheim, Darmstadt, Francfort, Worms, Mayence, Wiesbaden, Mulhouse, Bale, and the Rhine, &c.

(CHEMIN DE FER DE L'EST.) *Place de la Bastille.—No. 4.*

**ROUTE** to Fontenay, St. Maur, Champigny, La Varenne, Vincennes, &c.

**ORLEANS RAILWAY.**
(CHEMIN DE FER D'ORLEANS ET DU MIDI.)
*Boulevard de l'Hopital.—No. 6.*

**ROUTE** to Bretigny, Etampes, Orleans, Vendome, Blois, Tours, Angers, Nantes, Napoleon-Vendee, St. Nazaire, Poitiers, La Rochelle, Rochefort, Angoulême, Bordeaux, Montauban, Cette, Bayonne, Pau, Narbonne, Toulouse, Madrid, and to Spain, Portugal, &c.

**LYONS & MEDITERRANEAN RAILWAY.**
(PARIS A LYON ET LA MEDITERRANEE.)
*Boulevard Marais. No. 5.*

**ROUTE** to Brancy, Montargis, Melun, Fontainebleau, Montereau, Sens, Joigny, Auxerre, Laroche, St. Florentin, Tonnerre, Montbard, Verrey, Dijon, Auxonne, Beaucaire, Belfort, Beaune, Chalons-s-Saone, Macon, Belleville, Villefranche, Lyons, Chasse, Vienne, St. Rambert, Tain, Valence, Livron, Montelimar, Orange, Sorgnes, Avignon, Tarascon, Nîmes, Montpellier, Cette, Arles, St. Chamas, Rognac, Marseilles, Grenoble, Culoz, Geneva, Lucerne, Aix-les-Bains, Chambery, Chamounix, St. Michel, Susa, Turin, Milan, Trieste, Rome, Naples, Toulon, Cannes, and Nice; also, the Overland Route to Egypt, India, &c., *via* Marseilles, and Alexandria, &c.

LONDON:
59, FLEET STREET, E.C.

MANCHESTER:
ALBERT SQUARE.

# BRADSHAW'S

YEARLY LIST OF

# RAILWAY GUIDES HANDBOOKS,

## BRITISH AND CONTINENTAL,

*Published by WM. J. ADAMS (Bradshaw's British and Continental
Guide Office), 59, Fleet Street, E.C.*

## MONTHLY.

**BRADSHAW'S Railway and Steam Navigation Guide for Great Britain and Ireland,** with
Splendid Railway Travelling Map of Great Britain & Ireland, on the 1st of every Month.  Price 6d.

**BRADSHAW'S Railway Guide for England, Wales, and Scotland,** giving the Official Time Tables
of all the Railways (abridged from the larger Sixpenny Edition).  Price 3d.

**BRADSHAW'S Railway Time-Table Sheet** (of all the Railways), for the use of Railway Stations,
Club Houses, Hotels, Public and Private Offices, &c.  Price 3d.

**THE LONDON AND PROVINCIAL BRADSHAW—"A Through Communication Guide."**
ALPHABETICAL and TABULAR ARRANGEMENT shewing the entire Train Service between the
METROPOLIS and all parts of ENGLAND, WALES, and SCOTLAND, with ALPHABETICAL List of
RAILWAY FARES, &c.  Price 4d.  An Excellent Map, &c.

**BRADSHAW'S Continental Railway Steam Transit and General Guide for Travellers in Europe.**
Price 1s. 6d., with Map of the Continent.

**BRADSHAW'S Special Continental Railway Guide and Descriptive Handbook for the whole**
of Europe, including Turkey, Algeria, and Overland Routes to India, with Railway Map of Europe,
and Plans of the principal Continental Cities.  Price 3s. 6d. cloth.

# ANNUALS.

## ANNUALLY.

BRADSHAW'S Complete Guide through Paris and its Environs. Cloth, 2s. 6d. With a Splendid Map and numerous Artistic Steel Engravings, illustrative of the principal objects of attraction.— "*This well-arranged and convenient Handbook to the French Metropolis, pronounced unanimously by the British, Continental, and American Press as a most meritorious production, whether it be regarded for the full, clear and judicious compilation or its unsurpassed cheapness—embracing, as it does, not only all that can be seen in this beautiful City and Environs—but also for the useful and comprehensive instruction it imparts. Every line of Bradshaw's Paris Guide is not only useful, but really practical information of the greatest value to the British and American visitor. The pictorial illustrations are admirable—the map is worthy the world-wide fame of Bradshaw—the lowness of the price is within the reach of every class of visitors—indeed, the purchase of this Guide Book will tend much to economise the expenses of a trip to Paris.*"

BRADSHAW'S Continental Phrase Books—(handy and convenient for the pocket)—for the use of Travellers and Students, in English, French, German, Italian and Spanish. Bound in cloth, 1s. each.

    BRADSHAW'S Anglo-French Phrase Book—One Shilling.

    BRADSHAW'S Anglo-German Phrase Book—One Shilling.

    BRADSHAW'S Anglo-Italian Phrase Book—One Shilling.

    BRADSHAW'S Anglo-Spanish Phrase Book—One Shilling.

Each of these Books contains a Vocabulary of the most useful words, carefully translated—the modes of addressing the Dignitaries of England, France, Germany, Italy, and Spain—Letters, Notes, Invitations, &c.

BRADSHAW'S (Illustrated) Handbook to GERMANY, NORTH & SOUTH—forming a complete Guide to the whole Country, including all the Spas and places of resort—adapted to the Railway System, with Maps, Town Plans, &c., &c. 5s. cloth.

BRADSHAW'S (Illustrated) Handbook to NORTH and SOUTH ITALY, including ROME, with Maps and Town Plans, &c. Cloth, 7s. 6d.

BRADSHAW'S (Illustrated) Handbook to SPAIN, by Dr. CHARNOCK, F.S.A., with Maps, Town Plans, &c. Cloth, 7s. 6d.

BRADSHAW'S (Illustrated) Handbook to FRANCE, with Maps, Town Plans, &c. Cloth, 5s.

BRADSHAW'S (Illustrated) Handbook to BELGIUM and the RHINE, with Maps, Town Plans, &c. Cloth, 5s.

BRADSHAW'S (Illustrated) Handbook to SWITZERLAND, with Maps, Town Plans, &c. Cloth, 3s. 6d.

BRADSHAW'S New Pedestrian's Route Book for SWITZERLAND, CHAMOUNI, and the ITALIAN LAKES; with numerous Pass, Road, and Local Maps, and General Map of the Country, including an HOTEL and PENSION GUIDE, and full descriptions of all the best centres for Excursionists. Price 5s. cloth.

BRADSHAW'S (Illustrated) Handbook to the TYROL; or, Notes for Travellers in the Tyrol, and Vocabulary; with Illustrations from original sketches, Maps, &c., &c. Cloth, 2s. 6d.

BRADSHAW'S Handbook to the TURKISH EMPIRE, in 2 Parts, 7s. 6d. each, with Maps, &c.

    PART I.—TURKEY in EUROPE.
    PART II.—SYRIA and PALESTINE, &c., with Maps, &c.

BRADSHAW'S Guide through Normandy and the CHANNEL ISLANDS, with Maps. Price 1s. 6d. Stiff wrapper.

BRADSHAW'S (Illustrated) Handbook to BRITTANY, by the Rev. C. W. HUGHES, with Notices of the Physical Features, Agriculture, Language, Customs, History, Antiquities, and Sporting, with a complete Itinerary and Guide to all the objects of interest, with Maps. 2s. 6d. each.

BRADSHAW'S (Illustrated) Guide and General Handbook for **GREAT BRITAIN AND IRELAND,** with Maps of Great Britain and Ireland, Plans of Cities and Towns, and original Sketches, &c. Complete in cloth, 5s. 6d.

BRADSHAW'S Illustrated Sections of GREAT BRITAIN and IRELAND:—

    SECTION I.—Comprises a Descriptive Guide through London and Environs, and a comprehensive Handbook of the South Eastern, London Chatham and Dover, North Kent, the South Western, the Brighton and South Coast Railways; the Channel Islands, and Isle of Wight. Price 1s.

      *To the above is added the Tourist and Summer Arrangements of all the Railways.*

    SECTION II.—Comprises a Descriptive Guide and Handbook to the London and North Western, Great Western, Bristol and Exeter, North and South Devon, West Cornwall, South Wales, West Midland, &c., &c,, Railways; together with Tours through Ireland. Price 1s.

      *To the above is added the Tourist and Excursion Arrangements of all the Railways.*

    SECTION III.—Comprises a Descriptive Guide and Handbook to the London and North Western, North Stafford, Lancashire and Yorkshire (Western Section), Ayrshire, Caledonian, the Railways of Scotland. Guide to the English and Scotch Lakes. Price 1s.

      *To the above is added the Tourist and Summer Arrangements of all the Railways.*

    SECTION IV.—Comprises a Descriptive Guide and Handbook to the Great Northern, the Midland Counties, Manchester, Sheffield and Lincolnshire, Great Eastern, Lancashire & Yorkshire (Eastern Section), North Eastern, Stockton and Darlington, North British Railways, &c., &c., Price 1s.

      *To the above is added the Tourist and Summer Arrangements of all the Railways.*

BRADSHAW'S Itinerary of Great Britain, for Railway and Telegraphic Conveyance to and from every Town, Village and Parish containing a Population of 500 and upwards, shewing the Mode of Access, Mileage, &c., from the Metropolis ; the Nearest Station, and distance therefrom to adjacent Towns, Villages, Parishes, &c. ; the Situation, Counties and Population ; a General Railway Station List, and Complete Electric Telegraph Directory and Map of Great Britain. Price 2s. 6d. stiff covers ; 4s. cloth.

BRADSHAW'S Railway Manual, Shareholder's Guide, and Official Directory, contains the History and Financial Position of every Railway Company, British, Foreign, and Colonial : Statistic Powers and other data to the close of the year ; Railway Interest in Parliament, &c., &c. Alphabetical Arrangement of the whole Administrative and Executive Staff of all the Railway Companies of the United Kingdom, with large Railway Map, &c. Cloth, 12s.

# INDIA.

*New and Improved Edition, cloth, 5s.—Post, 5s. 6d.*

## BRADSHAW'S THROUGH ROUTES.—OVERLAND GUIDE AND

HANDBOOK to India, Turkey, Persia, Egypt, Australia, New Zealand, China, Japan, the Cape, and Mauritius. A Complete Traveller's Manual. How to Reach and how to Live in the Three Presidencies of India and Australian Settlements. This indispensable little Handbook contains *Twenty-five Outward and Homeward through Routes between Great Britain—her Indian and Australian Dependencies,* with Practical and Interesting Descriptive Guides to each Route. The Railway Time Tables of India ; Steam Navigation, Coasting, Coach, and other Conveyances ; Telegraph Communications ; Tables of Distances ; Tabular Forms of Expenses ; Time of Journey, &c. Advice to the Eastern Traveller—Hints as to the Purchase of Outfit—Luggage—Currency, &c. ; with a most useful Vocabulary of Hindostanee ; illustrated with MAPS of INDIA—the various ROUTES to INDIA, &c. Panorama of the Nile. Plans of Calcutta, Madras, Bombay, and Constantinople, and other illustrations.

## HEALTH RESORTS, WATERS, AND CLIMATES.

*Now Re-issued, Second Edition, enlarged, 7s. 6d.*

## THE CONTINENT, Considered chiefly in a Climatic and Remedial Point of

View. Comprising General and Medical Notices of the CHIEF PLACES of RESORT in FRANCE, ITALY, and GERMANY, with Remarks on the Influence of Climate and Travelling, and Meteorological Tables. By EDWIN LEE, M.D. (Member of several Medical Academies and Societies) &c.

BY THE SAME AUTHOR,

BATHS of SWITZERLAND and SAVOY, with Remarks on the action of Mountain Air, 3s. 6d.
BATHS of FRANCE, Fourth Edition, 3s. 6d.
THE BATHS of GERMANY, Fourth Edition, 7s.
BATHS of NASSAU, New Edition, 2s. 6d.
WATERING PLACES of ENGLAND, Fourth Edition, 7s. 6d.
HOMBURG and NAUHEIM, 1s.
NICE and its CLIMATE, Second Edition, 3s. 6d.
NICE et son CLIMAT, Second Edition, 2s 6d.
NOTICES of MENTON and SAN REMO, 3s. cloth ; New Edition.
HYERES and CANNES, 2s. cloth ; New Edition.
HEALTH RESORTS of the SOUTH of FRANCE (Hyeres, Cannes, Pau, Biarritz, &c.) Second Edition, 3s. 6d.
SPAIN and its CLIMATES, 3s. 6d.

London :—WM. JAMES ADAMS, No. 59, Fleet Street, E.C.